From Slocan to Hong Kong

An Architect's Journey

Cover photograph by Dr. Neville Poy

Order this book online at www.trafford.com
or email orders@trafford.com

Most Trafford titles are also available at major online book retailers.

Print information available on the last page.

ISBN: 978-1-4251-2244-7 (sc)

Trafford rev. 01/02/2018

 www.trafford.com
North America & international
toll-free: 1 888 232 4444 (USA & Canada)
fax: 812 355 4082

James H. Kinoshita

From Slocan to Hong Kong

An Architect's Journey

Contents

Acknowledgements

Information about the internment of the Japanese Canadians during the war was taken from *The Enemy That Never Was*, by Ken Adachi.

I wish to thank my mother for searching out and reproducing photographs of myself when I was young, as well as one showing my grandfather in the early days. I also want to thank Cora, my sister–in–law, who gathered the information about my grandfather's history in Japan and about how he came to Canada.

I owe further thanks to my daughters Yuri, Reimi and Hiromi for reading the initial draft manuscript and making valuable suggestions for revisions. Finally, I am grateful to my wife for giving me her wholehearted support and for being so patient with my spending so much time at the computer.

Introduction: The sign of the cock

Orientals link the year of birth to a 12-year cycle, with each year representing a particular animal symbol whose origin and meaning go back to ancient India and China. A legend says that on a certain New Year's Day, Buddha called all the animals of the world to him and promised that anyone who paid him homage would have a year named after him. Twelve animals came in this order: the rat, ox, tiger, rabbit, dragon, snake, horse, sheep, monkey, cock, dog, and boar. According to popular belief, people born in the year of a certain animal will have the traits peculiar to that animal.

I was born in 1933, the year of the cock. *The Japanese Fortune Calendar*, by Reiko Chiba, characterizes people born in the year of the cock as follows:

> Cock-year people are deep thinkers. They are always busy and devoted to their work. They always want to do more than they are able, and if they undertake a task beyond their abilities, they are disappointed when they discover they are unable to fulfill their obligations. People born in

this year are eccentric, and it is their eccentricity that prevents them from what is known in Japan as "roundness" in their relationship with others. Cock people always think they are right and that they know what they are doing. They do not trust other people and prefer to do what they like, alone. Their outward attitude and presentation is that of an adventurous spirit, but inwardly they have little gift for high adventure and are filled with nonsensical plans that never mature.

Although they are ambitious, for all their deep thinking they are not far-seeing and are somewhat improvident, for their fortunes resemble waves: sometimes they are wealthy, sometimes not. They are selfish and unheeding of other people's feelings and have a habit of speaking out directly whenever they have something on their minds. They are not at all shy and are quite brave when the occasion calls for it. Other people find the cock people interesting, but unless they are careful, cock people will lose the good opinion of others.

Another book, *Animals of the Chinese Zodiac*, by T. C. Lai, tells a different story:

The cock represents the tenth of the symbolical animals of the Twelve Terrestrial Branches. It was traditionally a timekeeper and symbolic of labour and trade because these depended on timeliness for their success. The cock does not stop functioning because of storm or rain. It has five virtues, namely,

(1) it excels in elegance because it wears a head-dress, to wit, its crest,

(2) it can be militant because it has a spur on each foot,

(3) it is brave because it dares to defy its enemies,

(4) it is beneficent because where there is food it does not fail to inform its comrades,

(5) it is trust-worthy because it keeps time.

Although it is impossible for all those born in the year of the cock to have the same characteristics, it is rather interesting that in my case, much of what is described above does come close to my character.

Whether I am a deep thinker or not is debatable, but I am always busy and devoted to work. However, I do not consider myself to be eccentric. My wife, Lana, tells me that I always feel I am right and never admit or apologize when I am wrong. I do prefer to do things on my own, though this is not because I don't trust other people. As to my outward adventurous spirit that never matures, maybe the description is right. I like to be adventurous, and do things like going to the North Pole, but I also want the comfort and safety of a Russian icebreaker, without risk or hardship. I am not selfish, but Lana tells me that I am self-centred and unheeding of other people's feelings. For example, if Lana is cold, I am unaware of it because I am not cold.

I do not feel I excel in elegance: I present myself rather plainly and simply. Maybe my wife takes that honour. I am certainly not militant—in fact, I am a firm believer in peace. But I do keep time.

Perhaps it was the need to discover myself that urged me to write my memoir. By reflecting on your own past, you become much clearer about who you are, what you are and why you are here. Or perhaps it was also to gain a kind of immortality; certainly I wanted to leave my future generations a record of my life and ancestry so that they would be aware of their heritage. It was especially important to me to describe my professional life. My career as an architect has been a kind of journey—from the small city of Slocan, British Columbia, where I did much of my early schooling, to Hong Kong, where I worked on many large building projects.

What finally triggered my writing of this memoir was hearing from a former classmate of mine. Bernard Dewe Mathews, whom I had met when we were both in the Advanced Management Program at Harvard Business School, sent me his memoir, *Blowing My Own Trumpet*. I found it very interesting and realized that everyone has a story to tell. That was when I said to myself, *Why not write my own?*

1

A cock is born

My family name, Kinoshita, in Japanese means "under the tree." Therefore, a cock was born under the tree. To my own name, and to that of each of my siblings, my father attached an individual meaning that also related to the family name. As I was the firstborn, I was named Hajime, written with the character 一 and translated as first or beginning. I was joined two years later by my brother, Gene, and because he was the second son born "under the tree," the character for his name contains the figure two 仁. My sister was named Aki 明子, which means bright, in order to bring light into the shade "under the tree." Next came Michi 道代, which means a road or path, in order to lead and welcome people into the family "under the tree." The last son, Kiyomitsu 清光, also means bright: "to light up the welcome."

I was born in Vancouver, a third-generation Canadian of Japanese origin. I was a happy child in my early days. My world revolved around "Little Tokyo," that section of East Vancouver along Powell Street where most of the Japanese living in Vancouver were concentrated. At first we lived on Alexander Street, a

Pictured left: The house at 350 Alexander Street, where I was born.
At the right: Father in 1934 with JHK and our dog, Johnny.

block away from Powell, in a two-storey wooden house with a lawn in the front. We had a large Collie dog, called "Johnny," that I adored. He was very gentle and patient with me. He was bigger than me so I was able to sit on his back as if I were riding a horse. One day when he was running after our car on the road, he suddenly collapsed due to a heart attack. I was very sad to lose my faithful companion.

Near our home was a large warehouse with a huge driveway and parking space. On weekends and holidays when the parking lots were empty, we went there to roller-skate and ride our bicycles. Even today, this area has huge warehouses, as it is close to the railway and the waterfront.

My father loved to drive the car. We frequently went on outings to the beach at Kitsilano or to catch crabs at White Rock, which was a very rocky, rather than a sandy, beach. Once at White Rock, my mother handed me a bag without telling me what was in it. I held the bag carefully as I was afraid of something moving inside the bag. Suddenly something pinched my finger very hard; I cried out in pain and let go of the bag. A huge crab came scrambling out of the bag.

One rainy day—and it seems to always rain in Vancouver—my mother took my brother Gene and me to town. Walking home, we had to cross a very busy intersection. Buses, trams, taxis and cars were moving in all directions. My mother was carrying Gene, as he was quite young, and held my hand as we waited for the traffic light to change. As it changed, I let go of my mother's hand and suddenly ran across the street. Wham! I was hit by a car turning the corner and was knocked unconscious. The next thing I remember was being carried home by my mother. One side of my face was completely swollen and I could not open my eye. At home, my mother applied a piece of raw steak to my blue and black swollen face, until a doctor came to see me. Luckily I was just badly bruised with no broken bones. After that, I was told to always hang on to someone when

Mother with baby JHK.

crossing a street.

At the age of six, I entered Strathcona School. I do not remember any of my classmates, but the class photograph shows a large number of Oriental students, because the school was located on the fringe of both the Japanese and Chinese communities.

I was anxious to participate in class activities and recall one incident when I volunteered to sing " Jingle Bells" for our class Christmas party. At the party, I started to sing " Jingle Bells" as I knew it. When I finished, there was silence, and everyone looked at me strangely. The teacher said that I only sang the chorus and asked if I could now sing the whole song. As I looked confused and embarrassed, the teacher and the whole class sang "Jingle Bells" with me joining in with the chorus. When I told my mother about what had happened, she consoled me and taught me the words for the whole song. I should have told her about my participation in the party beforehand and avoided the embarrassing incident.

Every day, after coming home from Strathcona School, I had to attend the Japanese school. I hated it. Why were my "*Hakujin*" (Caucasian) friends playing and enjoying themselves while I was forced to do more studies at the Japanese school? The teachers in the Japanese school were very strict and we were afraid of them. We had to learn everything from memory, which was very boring.

One day in class, I needed to use the bathroom and raised my hand to get permission. The teacher deliberately ignored my raised hand and continued to write on the blackboard, probably to teach me not to disturb her during class. I was getting desperate, however, and started to wave my hands frantically, while she became even more determined to ignore me. I finally could not wait, but afraid as I was to go out of the classroom without permission, I ended up wetting in my trousers. Everybody looked at me and I felt so embarrassed that I wished I could just disappear. Finally, the teacher noticed what had happened and told me in an embarrassed tone that I was excused, and to go home.

I could never write Japanese characters properly. One day as I was struggling with my writing, a boy named Kenji said, "Here, let me show you," and proceeded to write the most beautiful character, bold and full of life and vigour, which put my feeble effort to shame. I was very impressed with his skill and talent. A few years ago, in Vancouver on Powell Street, I went to a barber with my father. As I entered the barbershop, the barber recognized me and said, "Aren't you Hajime from our Japanese School?" I remembered that he was the same Kenji that had taught me calligraphy properly, and I wondered why such a talented young man ended up as a barber.

Sometime later, we moved to live upstairs at the fish and meat market that my maternal grandfather owned on Powell Street. Across the street was a Chinese restaurant called Fuji Chop Suey, which was also owned by my grandfather. To the east was a general store owned by my grandfather's older brother. A block away was a large playground with the United Church across the far end of the playground. A couple of blocks south of the playground was Strathcona School where I attended first and second grades. A block away, to the north of the playground, was the Japanese School that we had to attend after coming home from Strathcona.

There is one incident in my early life that I feel guilty about to this day. My brother Gene and I went along Powell Street to a shop to buy some candies. The shop was open to the street with many counters displaying rows of colourful candies. We strolled in and had a wonderful time choosing the candies. There was no one around, neither customers nor the proprietress. We finally selected the candies and waited for the proprietress to show up so we could pay. We waited for a long time but she did not appear. We shouted and banged on the counter to attract her attention but still no one came. We looked at each other, shrugged our shoulders and started to stroll out of the store, looking backwards to see if she would appear or not. Once on the street, we ran home, happy that we had gotten the candies for free.

As we were enjoying the candies, my mother came in to ask where we'd gotten them. "Er," we said, "there was no one there. It wasn't our fault; we tried to pay but no one came out. We weren't trying to cheat—it just happened like that."

It was all to no avail. She immediately hauled us back by our ears to the candy store to apologize to the owner and to pay for the candies.

I was three years old when my father took me to Japan to introduce me

1936 – JHK onboard the Hikawa Maru on route to Japan.

to his parents. We took *Hikawa Maru*, a Nippon Yusen Kaisha ship that sailed regularly from Vancouver to Yokohama. I had never been on such a large ship. I was afraid to be left alone in the dark cabin to sleep when my father went to have his dinner. The door to the cabin had louvers that filtered light from the corridor into the cabin and cast the shadows of anyone passing by the door. I could hear people talking and imagined shapes of terrible demons emerging through the louvers. I did not like any of the food on the ship and all I ate was *oni giri*, white rice wrapped in seaweed, throughout the trip. On the ship I wore a beret and a sailor's outfit to the delight of the crew.

In Japan, in my father's village of Kawaminami, in Shigaken, near Kyoto, I was thoroughly pampered by my grandparents. I was given a toy pedal car. I was thrilled with it and went all over the place. I remember distinctly that my grandmother had huge sagging breasts. Why I should remember that, I do not know; perhaps it was the Japanese habit of taking a bath together. The colour of my hair at that age was ginger, so people in Japan would frequently ask my father whether his wife was a Caucasian.

As far as I can recall, I enjoyed my first visit to Japan. Little did I realize then that I would not return until 24 years later.

Grandfather Maikawa in 1967.

14

2

From Japan to Canada

My father, Zenichi Kinoshita, was born on October 18, 1903, and went to Canada when he was 14 years old. He was the only son of Hisakichi and Masu Kinoshita, who come from Kawaminami Village, near Hikone, along the shore of Lake Biwa in Shiga Ken. My father has a younger sister, Hisako, who is still living in a village called Kawachi, near Hikone. Now that I live in Hong Kong, I visit her from time to time.

My grandfather, Hisakichi Kinoshita, was born on July 3, 1877. He was a farmer in Honjo, close to Kawaminami. Horse racing was quite popular in those days and my grandfather bred some racehorses. One day, when they went to Kyoto to see one of his horses race, their house was destroyed by fire. My father, who was four at that time, was left at home with my grandfather's brother, and fortunately his life was spared. The fire was probably caused by the rice straw they used as fuel for cooking, as the straws tend to continue burning unnoticed even after they appear to have been extinguished. My grandfather needed money to rebuild his house, so he decided to go to Canada. He sold his racehorses and his rice farm and left his family in his brother's care, telling them that he would not return until he earned enough money to rebuild his house.

In 1907, my grandfather went to Yokohama to get on a ship bound for Canada, but he didn't know how to obtain the ticket to board the ship or how to go through the proper procedure to pass immigration. Fortunately, a family that was sailing to Canada was able to help him. One of their sons had taken ill and had to be left behind, so grandfather tagged along as their "son."

In Canada he found that making money was not as easy as he thought. He worked hard as a fisherman, lumberman and even a whaler. A few years later, he was able to start sending money to Japan and, in 1915, he returned to Japan, bought a house in Kawaminami and renovated it.

Because my grandfather wanted to buy back their farmland and save money for retirement, he returned to Canada in 1918, this time taking my father with him. They landed in Victoria and went north to where my father worked as a cook's helper in the bunkhouse of a whaling company. When the season was over, they came to Vancouver and my grandfather told my father to learn English by working as a houseboy. His English was so poor that after three days as a houseboy, he was forced to attend Henry Hudson School in Kitsilano but had to start from grade one. He was terribly embarrassed, for at 15 years of age, he was much bigger than the other pupils.

At 18, my father went to work for my maternal grandfather's Maikawa store. It was a store that sold fish and meat, so he soon mastered how to fillet fish while saving the precious roe, how to grind fish for making Kamaboko (fish cake), how to shuck oysters, how to cut meat properly and how to serve customers courteously.

In 1923 my father returned to Japan to report for military service, and a huge earthquake occurred in Tokyo. Nervous about the bad omen, he went to see a fortune-teller who told him to leave Japan immediately, as his future there was dark. So he skipped military service, returned to Canada and continued to work for Maikawa.

When grandfather wanted him to return to Japan in 1926, my father refused to go back. A year later, my grandfather again asked my father to return, but my father replied that he would not go back to Japan and would make Canada his home. How different my life would have been if my father had returned to Japan.

The custom in Japan is for the eldest son to inherit the family property. As my father was the only son, and since he wanted to remain in Canada, my grandfather had to make alternative arrangements for the beneficiary of his property. As Hisako, my father's younger sister, was married to the Yamamoto family, the Kinoshita and the Yamamoto families negotiated for Osamu, the younger brother of the Yamamoto family to be adopted by the Kinoshita family and to change his name to Kinoshita. Osamu Kinoshita still lives in the house of my grandparents in Kawaminami and carries the family emblem of the Kinoshitas.

My father was a good-looking man with a long face. He dressed himself well and enjoyed gambling, especially horse racing, a trait he may have inherited from his father. However, he did not play for high stakes but gambled mainly for the excitement. Even when he played Mah Jhon or Kaji, a Japanese card game, he would insist upon a small stake, even if it were in pennies. He also enjoyed driving, which he had learned at the time he went to work for my maternal grandfather. Even later in his life, he would still drive from Vancouver to Las Vegas for a bit of Black Jack. He still enjoys a drink but, like many Orientals, cannot hold his liquor very well. He can fall asleep anywhere, even at a funeral service, where he sometimes disturbs the service by snoring loudly.

My mother, Yoshiko Maikawa, was born in Vancouver, B.C., on April 21, 1912. She is the third of five children. Her elder sister, Eiko, passed away in Rev-

17

elstoke in 1998, and her elder brother, Sadao, passed away in Toronto in 2005. Her younger sister, Fuji, is living in Edmonton and the youngest sister, Tomiko, passed away in Japan in 1974, just before she was about to move back to Canada.

My mother got along well with her brothers and sisters. She remembers washing the dog with her elder brother, Sadao, and recalls how he was always good to her. She did a lot of the work around the house, from cleaning to helping with the cooking. She also looked after her sister, Tomiko, who was always sickly. She was known as the "peacemaker" in the family because she never got upset and just smiled when things were not well. She was very close to her father—every time he wanted something, he'd always call for Yoshiko.

My mother went to preschool at the Presbyterian Church, attended Strathcona Elementary School and Brittania High School. Her favourite subject was mathematics. When she was 12 years old, she started taking private lessons in violin. She played in Japanese school concerts and joined the orchestra at Brittania High School. Uncle Sadao used to tease her about her screeching notes during violin practice. She also joined the CGIT (Canadian Girls in Training) and sang in the choir. She played on the grass hockey team in high school, participating in competitions with teams from other high schools.

Her parents were very strict and did not allow any contact with men, except when she was expected to entertain naval officers at the Hotel Vancouver. Sometimes she would be asked to play the violin at these events or dance and talk with them. However, she and the other girls she went with were always chaperoned. She doesn't remember being close to her mother. She remembers vividly that her mother used to get mad whenever she came home late from grass hockey practice.

My mother wanted to be a nurse and tried to convince her parents that she shouldn't get married until she was 21, but they wouldn't listen to her. When she finished high school, she took a business course, but three months after she started the course, the store got very busy and she had to help. When she tried to go back to school after the rush, she was told that she couldn't because all arrangements had been made for her to marry my father. She would never forget that day. She was taught to be obedient and to do what she was told: "Whether you wanted to or not, you had to do it." She was only 19.

My mother was the parent who brought us up, but I am sure she talked with my father about our education and our extracurricular activities, such as judo and kendo. She was the one we confided in and told our problems to. She was the one that taught us how to fold origami and to sing simple Japanese songs, like this one:

Caw, caw, the crows are calling.
Caw, caw, the crows are going home.

My parents emphasized the importance of education, especially after the Second World War started, saying. "They can take material things away from us but they cannot take things that are in our heads." They both encouraged us to study hard and were proud of us when we did well. My mother would never complain but kept things to herself—as the Japanese say, *"gaman suru."* She was a terrific cook and we all grew up enjoying her favourites: deep-fried chicken with special sweet and sour sauce, *oyako donburi* (chicken and egg on rice), *inari zushi* (sushi wrapped in fried tofu) and *miso* eggplant. My father would take over to prepare the *sashimi* (raw fish), which he loved.

My maternal grandfather was quite a character. He was born on March 14, 1880, in Maebara, very close to Hikone, Shiga Ken. His name was Sannosuke Maikawa and he was the third son in his family. In 1904, he decided to come to Canada to join his brother, who was working on the railroad. Intending to sail to Canada, he boarded a freighter from Japan but took the wrong boat and ended up in South America.

Without any money to pay for passage from South America to Canada, he stowed away on a ship going to the United States, and eventually ended up in Seattle. He was caught along the way, but the Captain couldn't do anything about it, so Sannosuke was made to work in the kitchen. After he arrived in Seattle, he had no idea where his elder brother was except that he worked on the railway. With this in mind, he started to walk along the railway and, after a patient search, finally located his brother. It was a happy reunion after all the adventure. He also worked on the railway and later to went to work in a sawmill.

In 1908 he returned to Japan to get married to Uta Bando. He returned to Canada with his bride and started a family. One night at the sawmill, he had a bad dream and, feeling nervous, reported in sick. Nonetheless, he decided to show up for a short time to teach his substitute how to get the work done. While he was demonstrating, he accidentally cut off the ring finger and baby finger of his right hand. Because of this accident, he couldn't go back to work at the sawmill; but he still needed to feed his family and opened a restaurant serving *sukiyaki* and *udon*. He later sold the restaurant and built an apartment building near the corner of Templeton and Powell Streets. Behind the apartment, he built the house where my mother was born. That house is still standing today.

When the First World War broke out, business was poor, and he was forced to sell the house and apartment building. At that time, he already had four children and, knowing that even in bad times people still had to eat, he decided to open a fish and meat market at 333 Powell Street. He would go down to the dock every morning to buy fresh fish, pick out the fish and, using his wagon, haul them by hand to the store.

The store soon began to prosper. He was able to buy the house on 350 Alexander Street and moved his family there. His brother had advised him to live close to his business, so the house was ideal from that point of view and was

Grandfather Maikawa in front of his store at 333 Powell Street.

also near to Japanese School, where his children attended. He decided to buy the building that he rented for his store (on 333 Powell Street) and set up an office and living quarters on the second floor. He built a concrete building at the back of the store and used the area to start producing *kamaboko* or fish cakes. He brought in a man from Japan to make the fish cakes.

It was about this time that my father joined him and eventually managed the store after he married my mother. Grandfather Maikawa and his wife then retired to Japan and settled in Hikone where he became mayor. He would return to Vancouver every year, from November to January, to help during the busy season—Christmas and New Year's.

Grandfather Maikawa always liked to try new business ventures, one of which was an oyster farm on Vancouver Island. He hired someone from Japan to

1935 – Grandfather Maikawa at Fanny Bay with his oysters.

check the waters around Fanny Bay for its suitability for cultivating oysters. He then imported some oyster seeds from Japan and had them planted around Fanny Bay. The oysters were shipped to Vancouver to be sold to individual customers and restaurants. The Fanny Bay oysters are still thriving and are now well known in both Canada and the United States.

Grandfather Maikawa then decided to open a Chinese restaurant, called *Fuji Chop Suey*, on Powell Street. Chinese restaurants were becoming very popular, not only amongst the Japanese community but also with Canadians. We were to enjoy many Chinese meals there. Every occasion was an excuse to have a feast there. I grew up eating chop suey and chow mein, which I still enjoy, although Lana teases me that they are not authentic Chinese food. To this day, however, I do not enjoy eating chicken feet. My grandfather later left the management of the

22

business to Tajiro Ogino, who had married my mother's elder sister.

His brothers also did well in Vancouver. His eldest brother, Tomikichi, owned T. Maikawa, a general store that specialized in clothing, including fur coats. They later sold rice, which they processed themselves. The second brother, Sadakichi, owned a gas station and a garage that my grandfather had financed. The younger brother, Bungoro, worked for Tomikichi at the T. Maikawa store. After Tomikichi had his family, he took them back to Japan and became the Mayor of Hikone. In his absence, Bungoro managed the store.

My grandfather was very hardworking and believed in self-reliance. At his store he made all the employees feel that they were part of a family, including my father. My father officially joined the family when he married my mother. Another employee, Tajiro Ogino, further enlarged the family by marrying the eldest daughter, Eiko.

Besides managing the store, my father was given other responsibilities. One was to entertain the officers of the Japanese shipping line Nippon Yusen Kaisha. The store was appointed as the chandler for the shipping line and it was part of that duty to entertain the ship's officers. Many a night we were kept awake by the boisterous singing from the party when we were living above the store. My father also took the officers on sightseeing tours of Vancouver, visiting places like Stanley Park and the suspension bridge at Capilano Canyon; sometimes I was lucky enough to be taken along.

My Maikawa grandfather built a large house in Hikone, big enough to accommodate his whole family, should they go to Japan. The house had a traditional Japanese living room as well as a Western-style living room with overstuffed sofas and a Marconi radio. It also had a well-kept Japanese garden with pine trees, rocks, stone lanterns and azalea plants. I was able to appreciate this when I visited him in Japan in 1960.

When the war started, the Canadian government confiscated all the properties and moved all the Japanese living within 100 miles of the West Coast to internment camps in the interior. My grandfather was angry that the Canadian government took away everything he had built up. He lost his fish and meat market on 333 Powell Street, a Japanese public bath and a house behind the bathhouse on 337 Powell Street, Fuji Chop Suey, his family home on 350 Alexandra Street and the oyster farm in Fanny Bay. He took the last ship to Japan that was to leave from Vancouver and spent the war years in Japan. When Japan lost the war and was occupied by US forces, MacArthur started to change a lot of policies, especially ones regarding the ownership of land.

In Japan my grandfather owned several houses as well as farmlands. A new decree came out that an individual could only own the house that he was living in and a minimal amount of farmland to till per person—enough to grow your own quota of rice and vegetables. As a result of these policies, most of his land was confiscated; this made him a very bitter man. He had lost his property in Canada and now he lost his property in Japan. After his wife died in 1961, he decided to come back and live in Canada. He was a natural farmer and had the patience and diligence to till our one acre of land in Slocan and grow huge healthy vegetables. Those we did not eat, he pickled in the traditional Japanese way, by stacking them in layers interspersed with handfuls of salt and weighing down the layers with a heavy stone.

It was during this process that he was struck down by a stroke, which paralysed him, and he was confined to a nursing home in Nelson until his death in 1973. During his life in Slocan, he loved fishing, hunting for *matsutake* mushrooms and, of course, gardening.

3

Internment

The Japanese attacked Pearl Harbor on December 7, 1941. Consequently, war was declared on Japan, and this profoundly affected the lives of every person of Japanese ancestry living in Canada. Japanese fishing boats were impounded and movement was controlled. Curfew was imposed from sunset to sunrise. We had to surrender our automobiles, radios and cameras. I possessed a camera that I treasured, and when I heard that I would have to surrender it, I hastily buried it in the lane between our buildings. If I were to go back and search for that camera today, I would probably still find it, albeit in a very rusty condition.

One day at Strathcona School, the teacher took me gently aside and told me that I did not have to go back to school. I felt lost and lonely because I did not understand why I was the only person leaving school in the middle of classes. There were encounters on the street with people calling me "Jap," but at that age, I was unsure about the meaning. Nonetheless, I could feel the hatred behind the remark.

As I was now idle during the day, my mother sometimes took me to the movies. One I remember well is a Charlie Chaplin movie in which he is starving in a log cabin surrounded by deep snow. He had nothing to eat so he took off his boots, unlaced the shoelaces and proceeded to eat it like spaghetti. I was amazed to see how he ate his shoelaces. Much later, I was to find out that the shoelaces were made of licorice candy. Fortunately, I didn't try to see how my own shoelaces tasted.

The curfew was most restrictive to my freedom. Living on top of the store, we did not have a traditional Japanese bath—ours was located in our old house on Alexander Street. I would go over there for my bath but sometimes I would finish past the curfew. I would have to sneak along the side of the dimly lit deserted alley while making sure the police did not see me. In a way it was an adventure for me. I missed going to the beaches and playing in Stanley Park. Although we were still able to go to these places with no restriction, my parents avoided public areas because of discrimination.

Canada at that time had a population of 11 million people. Those of Japanese descent numbered 23,000, and most were living in British Columbia with a third living in Vancouver, concentrated mainly on Powell Street. They had established a small community with their own Japanese school, a Buddhist temple, a kindergarten, a church, shops, restaurants, rooming houses, laundries, pool halls, gas stations, barbershops and bathhouses.

The Japanese had started to come to Canada in the late 19th and early 20th centuries. Their intension in coming to Canada had been to make money and then to go back to Japan to buy land or housing, but many ended up making their home in Canada. The first generation, called *Issei,* either kept their Japanese nationality or became naturalized Canadians. The second generation was called *Nisei,* and almost all of them were born in Canada. Both my grandparents came to Canada, which makes me third generation, or *Sansei.*

When the Japanese first came to Canada, they worked on the railway, in lumber camps, or in canneries. Later, when they were able to save some money and obtain licenses, many went into fishing. They concentrated around Steveston, a small fishing village outside Vancouver on the Fraser River. They became so successful that the government was pressurized into restricting fishing licenses to the Japanese. Many turned to farming along the rich and fertile Fraser Valley where, by hard work and determination, they also made a great success. Since they were able to catch the most fish and produce the best strawberries at low prices, the situation created strong resentment amongst many white Canadians. This resentment exploded when war was declared

When the war started, all the fear, resentment and jealousy held by the white community against the Japanese bubbled to the surface. Fishing boats were immediately confiscated and then auctioned *en masse*, selling at extremely low prices. The politicians and the unions saw this situation as an opportunity to get rid of the Japanese and finally were able to force the government to evacuate the Japanese.

Soon, all those of Japanese ancestry living within 100 miles of the coast were evacuated to internment camps located at various places in the interior of Canada. The people who were living outside of Vancouver were first collected at Hastings Park, where an annual show was held for livestock and agricultural products. The stables that usually held cows and other domestic animals were used to hold people. Some people were only given 24 hours to pack and move to Hastings Park. Any property they owned was expropriated by the government.

Many decided to sell their properties and possessions at a ridiculously low price. These people were then herded onto the train to be shipped to various internment camps. Each adult was allowed to take 150 pounds and each child 75 pounds. Personal items, such as furniture, clothes, and household equipment, were either left behind in the custody of the government or sold to the junk man who came around in his horse-drawn wagon to collect things from all those who

1942 – The family shortly before the internment. From left to right: Mother, JHK, Aki, Gene and Father.

were leaving. The wagons were a familiar sight and they must have done a roaring business. The people who sold their possessions, even at a very low price, were the lucky ones, because those who chose to entrust the government with their possessions soon saw their valuables plundered and ransacked.

We were quite fortunate in having a food store, and it was considered necessary for us to continue with our business; we were therefore one of the last families to leave Vancouver. In the middle of winter 1942, we arrived in a small town called Slocan City in the Kootenays, in the interior of British Columbia;

this was to be our home for many years. There was no permanent accommodation available so we initially had to share a tent with another family.

It was very cold, with three feet of snow outside. It happened to be the coldest winter in many years. There was no electricity or running water. The tent had a single wood-burning stove in the middle, and we all huddled around it. Toilets were outdoors, and we had to struggle through the snow and wait in line to use the bathroom. We ate in the local skating rink with long tables and bench seats on a dirt floor. Women and children ate first and the men ate later on.

After living in the tent for a while, which seemed like ages, we were able to get a cubicle in a two-storey bunkhouse, called Popoff Farm, on the outskirts of Slocan City. The bunkhouse was made up of many cubicles, each eight-feet square with six-foot high partitions, located on each side of a central corridor with a communal kitchen at one end and toilets at the other. Our family of five occupied one of the cubicles. Some mode of privacy was achieved by putting a piece of cloth across the opening to the cubicle. The cry of a baby, a mother scolding her child, or someone passing wind reverberated throughout the open partitions. There was no electricity. We used candles and coal oil lamps. There was no running water; it had to be fetched from a communal tap some distance off.

It was a time of great hardship for my parents, who had led a relatively easy life before the war. I was too young to feel whether or not life was hard, but I remember that I had to do many things I had never done before. One day for a special occasion, I was asked by my mother to kill a chicken. As I had no idea how to kill a chicken, I asked my mother how to go about it. She impatiently told me to get an axe and chop her head off. So off I went to look for an axe, and after finding it, I located a suitable stump on which to carry out the beheading. The chicken, however, was totally uncooperative and would not keep still long enough for me to chop her head off. After many attempts, I finally became impatient and wildly swung the axe, successfully decapitating the bird. But when the head came off the headless chicken flapped around so furiously that I got frightened and let it go. Off it went, flying through the air, spattering blood all over me. My mother regretted asking me to kill the chicken for she now had to wash my bloody clothes.

After several months in the cramped bunkhouse, we moved to a house in a small place called Roseberry. It was located near the other end of Slocan Lake, beyond New Denver, another heavily concentrated internment camp. The house was situated on the road near the lake. It was here that I would spend the most enjoyable time of my youth. The house itself was quite small, measuring 14 by 28 feet. It had three rooms—a central living/dining room with a wood-burning stove in the middle of the room and two rooms on each end for bedrooms.

When we first moved in we had to share the house with another family but even this was better than living in a bunkhouse. Eventually we added an extension to the back for the kitchen. The outhouse was outside at the back. Later we were able to add tar paper to the walls for insulation, as only one layer of board separated us from the elements.

Roseberry was surrounded by wilderness—the creek, the lake, the woods, and the mountains. The lake was well stocked with rainbow trout and the creeks with brook trout. There were plenty of bears and deer that would venture into our small settlement. When the moon rose over the mountains, the coyotes would begin to howl. It was an ideal vacation spot except we didn't—or couldn't—appreciate it at that time.

There was so much snow in the winter that I wanted to try skiing. I did not have any skis, so I decided to make them. I took two pieces of plank and stuck one end of the plank into a pot of boiling hot water. I then made a clamp to bend the softened end of the board into a curve. After it dried out, I released it from the clamp, trimmed the tip to a point, and added straps to tie onto my shoes. Of course I did not have ski boots or proper binding and had to do much improvisation. After I waxed these homemade skis with candle wax, I hiked up the snowbound logging road and skied down the steep slope. I did not know the correct technique for turning, so I usually came straight down ending up in a huge pile of snow at the bottom. The trouble with those skis was that after they got wet in the snow, the plank tended to spring back to it's original flat position, so the whole process of boiling and bending had to be repeated.

When Christmas approached, I went into the forest and cut a suitable fir tree. We decorated the tree by stringing together popcorn, cranberries, paper chains and origami hangings. And of course we hung our stockings up. I would wait in great anticipation for a surprise at Christmas. When we were living in Vancouver, my Uncle Sadao would give me a football or a toy gun that popped by punching a hole in the paper, all the sorts of thoughtful things that a boy would enjoy—not the clothes and shoes that mothers like to give. That Christmas, I was now 10 years old, and to my great joy, I received a pair of real skis. My parents must have felt sorry for me after seeing me struggle to make my skis. I really appreciated this gift because it must have been difficult, as well as costly, to obtain it in the internment camp.

We walked along a deserted railway track to go to school every day. It took longer in the winter with the deep snow, but in spring and autumn, it was fun to catch grasshoppers and butterflies along the track. In the autumn there were plenty of huckleberries and blueberries. I have never tasted huckleberries as good as those in Roseberry; they were big and juicy, and deep red in colour. Of course, you got the odd bear competing for the berries, but mostly they left us alone, as there was plenty of other food around for them.

Fishing was also a pastime I enjoyed very much. I either went up the creek to fish for brook trout or to the lake to fish for rainbow trout, which was usually caught at the mouth of the creek. Since we did not have a boat, we were not able to troll in the lake. Another favourite activity was mushroom picking. The mountain in this area abounds with a mushroom called *matsutake,* which is highly prized by the Japanese. It has a distinctive odour, and you can smell it when you are looking for it. It usually grows under a pine or hemlock tree and gives a faint telltale sign by raising a mound of the pine needles on the ground. When you carefully dig around this mound, you will find a family of *matsutake* mushrooms clustered together. Some are still buds, which are phallic in shape, and others are opened in the typical mushroom shape. You can tell that it is *matsutake* by its smell and by peeling the flesh—it peels off in strips. If it breaks or crumbles, it is not *matsutake.*

Picking mushrooms can be dangerous; there have been cases of people getting lost or accidentally falling into a canyon. However, it is such a wonderful feeling to walk in the woods where it is completely silent except for the wind making the trees sigh or the sound of a stream bubbling nearby. Occasionally in these deep dark woods, I would come across a deer or a mountain goat, but rarely a bear.

The men were encouraged to work doing manual labour, such as logging and building roads. My father went to work in a logging camp, but not being used to heavy labour, he found it too strenuous. For a time, he was unemployed but soon found the right opportunity. He was offered a job looking after a general store in Popoff Farm where we used to live in the bunkhouse; this time, though, we were able to live in a private house behind the store in the main compound of Popoff Farm, across the road from the internment camp. .

My father worked very hard at the store to make it a success. He introduced food that the Japanese community would enjoy, which was not available in other Canadian stores. He had a pickup truck that he would drive to other camps to sell products unique to the Japanese community. These trips were usually made in the evenings after the store closed for business. I think it was partly my

The internment camp at Popoff Farm; the bunkhouses are the large buildings in the middle.

father's nature to enjoy doing this extra work. He was very gregarious and enjoyed meeting people and chatting with them in the store. He was elected president of many associations, not only in Popoff but later in Slocan as well.

Mr. and Mrs. Popoff were Russian immigrants who moved to Canada when the Bolsheviks took over Russia. Mr. Popoff was an officer in the White Russian army and had to escape to Canada to avoid persecution from the Reds. There were other Russians living along the Slocan Valley, called the Doukhobors, who came to Canada in 1899 after being persecuted for refusing military service in Russia. They were peaceful farmers who provided fresh vegetables for the internees when we first came to the camp. They were to become a centre of attention when Canada tried to force conscription upon them: they protested by marching naked—men, women, and children. They escaped Russia for this reason and now they were again forced to be conscripted in Canada.

Life was now more comfortable. My sister Michi was born on May 21, 1943, followed by Kiyo on September 17, 1945. My father was happy at his work. Mr. and Mrs. Popoff treated us very well and we were to remain good friends until they both passed away while retired in Vancouver. Mr. Popoff was the farmer, milking the cow and feeding the chickens and pigs. Mrs. Popoff was the businesswoman, looking after the store. She left the care of the store to my father and he eventually bought the business from Mrs. Popoff.

I enjoyed my life in Popoff. We used to help Mr. Popoff collect the cows for milking or drive the cows to pasture after the milking. I even tried milking but without much success; it required quite a lot of skill as well as strength to draw the milk out. I also helped at the store doing deliveries after school. At least we did not have Japanese schools.

I attended a school in Popoff that was taught by former teachers with additional help provided by some high school students. I admired the creativity of some of the students, who had produced a beautiful garden at the side of the school. They took a small space and transformed it into a miniature garden with rocks, dwarf trees, bamboo, grass and sand, with a well-crafted bamboo fence around it. I wondered where such creativity came from; was it acquired or was it a natural Japanese characteristic? If it is the latter, why is it that I did not have it?

I took lessons in kendo, a Japanese competitive sport that uses a sword made of split bamboo pieces bound together for flexibility. The body is protected by a hard body armour, padded mittens and a padded helmet with a metal grill mask. The idea is to hit the opponent's body on certain designated points—the top or either side of the head, the throat, the wrists, or either side of the body. I never enjoyed this sport with its bashing away at one another, although it is supposed to build up your character and instil discipline. It really hurt when you got hit, especially on the exposed parts of the arm between the padded wrist and the body armour.

I made many friends in the camp, but now I have forgotten them all. This has been especially embarrassing when I have attended some function in Vancouver and someone has come up to me and called me by my name, with great familiarity, and I have not remembered him or her. They used to call me egghead, but I'm not sure whether it was because of the shape of my head, combined with a short haircut (which I still have), or because I did well in school. Anyway, I did not take it as a compliment.

Out of 21,000 Japanese living along the West Coast, about 18,000 people were evacuated to the internment camps in the British Columbia interior. The rest were moved to Alberta to work on the sugar beet farms, and a few moved to eastern Canada. About one quarter of those sent to internment camps were

Kendo—JHK is sitting fourth from the left.

housed in the Slocan Valley. From Slocan City, the camps were Bay Farm, Popoff and Lemon Creek. Twenty miles north on the other end of Slocan Lake were the camps of New Denver and Roseberry. Other camps were Tashme, Greenwood, Kaslo, and Sandon.

The camps did not have any barbwire. It wasn't needed because where could one escape to? There were very few Mounted Police in the camps as the Japanese community was very docile and obeyed orders. There were no riots or demonstrations—the people accepted their fate with the expression, "*Shikata ga nai*," meaning, "It can't be helped." We needed special permission to go to towns such as Nelson outside the controlled area, but we were free to travel between the camps. Once, when my mother got sick, I took a bus from Popoff to New Denver by myself to look for my father, who was there selling goods to the community. When I got there, I was able to locate him by looking for his pickup truck, even though it was already dark.

The forced evacuation left many bitter about their treatment. Most of the people were Canadians, either born in Canada or naturalized. The Japanese felt that they were being discriminated against. They asked why only the Japanese? If it were for the reason of war security, why was it that the Germans and the Italians were not placed in internment camps?

"*Shikata ga nai.*"

4

Slocan City

The US dropped atomic bombs on Hiroshima and Nagasaki. Japan surrendered. The war was over! The Japanese community living in the internment camps was given a choice of being repatriated back to Japan or moving to the east of the Rockies in Canada. Canada was imposing her policy of dispersing the Japanese to avoid the prewar situation of their concentration in British Columbia, especially around Vancouver. Some wanted to go to Japan after the treatment they had received in Canada, but my father strongly tried to persuade them that it was better to stay in Canada than to go back to a war-ravaged country. There was a lack of food, shelter and jobs, argued my father. Eventually 4,000 men, women and children moved to Japan.

Most people stayed and slowly settled in various parts of Canada. At first, we were not allowed to go back to Vancouver, but we were allowed to go later, in 1949. Many moved to Toronto and other places in the east. Today, Toronto has the highest concentration of Japanese in Canada. Those who were sent to Alberta had already settled down on their own sugar beet farms so they did not move.

Lemon Creek, Popoff and Bay Farm in the Slocan Valley were slowly abandoned and eventually returned to the bare fields that they were before the occupation. Some people remained in Slocan City and New Denver. They were mainly the old and infirm who did not wish to move, or were unable to do so.

We moved to Slocan City where my father opened a store after everyone had moved out of Popoff. We moved into a large one-storey house with an attic. The toilet was still an outhouse, but much later we had the luxury of an indoor toilet. Our house had a shingled roof and shingled sides, and sat on one acre of land where we grew strawberries and vegetables. There was an old cherry tree in the backyard. It was easy to pick the huge black Bing cherries when they got ripe because the branches became so overloaded with the weight of the fruit that they would hang down low enough for us to reach without ladders.

Slocan City was reputed to be the smallest incorporated city in Canada, if

The Slocan River.

Main Street of Slocan City.

not the world. In 1900, during the height of the silver boom, Slocan City was a thriving city with over 6000 people. It was located on the southern end of Slocan Lake in the Kootenay district and was surrounded by magnificent mountains and heavy forest. Its main industry was the sawmill located at the edge of the lake; the mill spoiled its potential as a resort. Most of the people here were working at the sawmill or were involved in logging. The city had a Main Street (which is still there) and both sides of the street were packed with many saloons and hotels. It is now a ghost town with shells of some of the buildings still remaining.

Like our family, some of the other Japanese living in the internment camps moved to Slocan City. They integrated well with the existing residents and made close friends. They became involved in trades such as making tofu, running a

Family in 1949. Back row, left to right: Gene, Mother, Shaw, Father and JHK. Front row, left to right: Aki, Kiyo and Michi.

barbershop or doing carpentry, while others joined the locals in driving logging trucks or working in the sawmill. In 1960 the population was 300—reduced to 299 when I left. I don't believe that any Japanese are left there, today; they either moved away or died off.

In 1988, after some outcry from citizens about the treatment of the Japanese in Canada during the war, the Canadian Government gave $21,000 as redress to every person subjected to internment "to acknowledge the injustices and to condemn the excesses of the past and to reaffirm the principles of justice and equality in Canada."

Could a situation like this occur again? If China and Canada were to go to war, would the Chinese living in Canada be subjected to the same treatment we received? I would hope not, but when racial discrimination lies smouldering under the facade of democracy and equality, a spark could easily ignite and cause a fire.

Due to the small number of students, each classroom in Slocan combined two or three grades into one classroom with one teacher teaching several grades. Mr. O'Neil was a tall rugged teacher with a long face; he looked more like a logger than a teacher. Despite his looks, he was a gentle and patient teacher whom I respected.

In the school year from 1947 to1948, I went to Nelson Junior High School. I tended to compare myself to other students, as each grade in Slocan was very small. As I did not want to rely on my parents to support me, I went to work as a houseboy with a family in Nelson. The father was the superintendent of the railroad and his house was located next to the railway station. I would help the lady of the house with the household duties, such as preparing breakfast or dinner, washing up after meals, tending the garden and looking after the house.

It was hard work from early in the morning to late at night, plus I was going to school during the day. I was not the master of my own time. I hated the housework, which robbed me of precious time for my studies. After half a year of being a houseboy, I'd had enough of the work, and my parents were able to find me lodging with an old Japanese couple living in Nelson. Every Sunday, the old couple would make a special meal of boiled whole chicken, which I love to this day. In order to support myself, I worked at a nearby Chinese restaurant during the busy weekends.

At school we were obliged to join the student army corps and wear army uniforms. We would practice drills and learn to shoot a rifle. One day after a drill, I dropped by the Chinese restaurant where I worked to proudly show my uniform. The Chinese were all shocked and expressed their strong disapproval. Here I was, a person of Japanese race, wearing a military uniform—no wonder they were shocked. I felt very embarrassed. To this day, I am strongly against war of any nature. My fellow students were very kind and friendly towards me, inviting me to their homes for dinner and to meet their parents. The teachers there were also very helpful in pointing out my strengths and weaknesses. My school year in Nelson is a very pleasant memory.

My next two school years were spent in Slocan. After a year in Nelson, I felt I was able to compete with the other students and I had missed Slocan. During these two years, the classes were slightly larger, but the school still had one teacher teaching several grades. There were about ten students in my grade, mostly girls.

There was one girl in the class with whom I fell madly in love. It was my first experience in love. Her name was Fern Cooper, and she was the daughter of a rancher living just outside of Slocan. She was tallish, with blonde hair, not particularly pretty but attractive in a rugged way. She was an outdoor girl who could shoot ducks and ride horses. Of course, in my circumstances I had no opportunity to shoot ducks or ride horses, so I felt that I had no way of competing

Slocan High School, 1949; JHK is in the back row, far left.

42

for her attention. I guess you would call it puppy love, and I was captivated by her. She probably knew that I mooned after her, but she did not respond to my attentions. On one occasion at school, we were asked to read out passages from *Romeo and Juliet*. I was to read the role of Romeo and Fern was to take the role of Juliet. When I got to the point where Romeo declares his love for Juliet, I choked so hard that I was not able to continue. Our teacher understood and quickly skipped the passage.

After school, I would help out at the store making deliveries, stocking up the shelves or carrying the heavy slabs of meat into the cooler. I enjoyed doing the deliveries with my bicycle, as I was able to go all over the place in Slocan. During the summer holidays, I started to work as a logger.

It was very hard work, as everything had to be done manually. The mountain was steep, and heavy machinery could not be used. After selecting a tree to cut, we would observe which way the tree was leaning and plan the best location for the tree to fall in order to make it easier to remove the log. Then, with an axe, we would cut a notch in the direction in which we wanted the tree to fall. With a two-man saw, we would manually saw the tree from the other side of the notch to make the tree fall in the right direction. This wasn't as easy as it sounds; usually the tree was on a steep slope, so one end of the saw would be close to the ground while the other end was way up in the air. After the tree was felled, the branches were trimmed; then the tree was cut into logs of predetermined length and dragged by horses to a holding position above a logging road so that it could be loaded onto trucks to be taken to the sawmill.

If the place being logged was too far away from home, we stayed at a camp in the mountains and came home only during the weekends. I was used to taking a bath every night so even when I was living in the camp, I would go down to the nearest stream and wash myself in the ice cold water. The other loggers used to tease me by saying, what is the use of washing yourself when you wear the same dirty shirt every day? I never ate as much as I did when I was logging. The physical activity and the fresh outdoor air made me very hungry. Even though logging was hard work, I enjoyed working outdoors in the wilderness and fresh air.

Another summer, I worked in the sawmill in Slocan. The logs were dumped into the lake where they would float inside a boom. Loggers balanced themselves on the floating logs to direct them to a conveyor, which would take the logs up to the sawmill. Balancing on logs in the water requires quite a skill and was often an exhibit at the local fair. One of the games was to challenge loggers to compete to see who could remain on the log the longest. The log was then mounted on a carriage where it was sliced into thin planks by a huge—and threatening-looking—circular saw. These planks would then slide into another pair of saws which were used to trim the bark off the two edges of the plank. Those planks that then went through the planer. The finished product would then be stacked with air spaces between each plank to dry them out.

It was hard and boring work. In logging you could set your own pace, but in the sawmill, the machine sets the pace and you have to keep up with it. Every night I would come home exhausted and would sprawl on the back porch to rest before taking off my heavy boots.

One summer, I worked in a lead mine near Slocan. It was a strange sensation to enter a world of darkness at dawn then emerge after dark. I seldom saw the sun all summer, except on weekends. The mine was a horizontal shaft located high in the mountains; one day in July, when we emerged from the mine, we were greeted by a foot of snow. Our job was to drill holes at the end of the horizontal tunnel. Then we packed the holes with dynamite, lit the explosives and retired to a safe place. After the explosion, when the smoke settled down, we would have to go in, muck out the ore onto carts and wheel them outside on tracks. It was dirty work—damp and sweaty.

I was happy to see the end of summer.

44

My brother and I would walk up to a small valley above Slocan, called Little Slocan, where we would catch so many brook trouts that everybody became tired of eating them. The valley was also full of huckleberries and blueberries. During the berry season we would meet quite a few bears. One day when Gene and I were hiking uphill to Little Slocan, our dog started to growl as we neared the crest of the hill. Just in front of us, staring at us, was a huge brown bear with her cubs. Afraid that our dog would attack the bears, I quickly grabbed hold of her. After a while, which seemed like ages, the bear slowly turned around and went away.

We also went up the Valhalla Mountains, located across Slocan Lake, to camp at a tiny lake called Cahill Lake near the top of the mountain. Few people went there because it was so remote, so the lake was always full of rainbow trout. Many years later, we were to return to this spot, with the family, to relive our childhood days. I often went mushroom picking in the forest where I enjoyed the solitude and closeness to nature. I must say that I have taken full advantage of the natural environment of Slocan.

There wasn't much to do socially in Slocan City. Winter was long and there was a lot of snow. The city had no cinema and no bars—only one coffee shop

Fishing at Cahill Lake.

attached to the only gas station—no hotels or motels, and no crime. There would be a dance once or twice a year at the Odd Fellow's Hall and we would go there to meet our friends. There was a dance on New Year's Eve, but we had to return home at the stroke of midnight to have our obligatory bowl of noodles, to signify long life. During those days, my father disapproved of us going to dances. Therefore we were delighted and surprised that after he retired and moved to Vancouver, he started taking dance lessons and enjoyed them.

I was still called Hajime, but many of my friends found it difficult to pronounce it and started to address me as "Hi Jimmy," which soon got shortened to "Jimmy." Therefore I decided to officially register my name as James. My name then became James Hajime Kinoshita.

For the final year of high school, I decided to go to a larger school to prepare myself for university and narrowed down the choice to King Edward High School in Vancouver. Once again, to support myself, I went to work as a houseboy with a family living close to the school. The father of the family was an architect, and while I was working there, I was able to observe what he was doing. This gave me the inspiration to become an architect. Because I did well in math, science and fine arts, the student counsellor also drew my attention to the architectural profession. Prior to my exposure to the architect's family as a houseboy, I did not know anything about architecture. It's strange how certain events shape one's life.

I was probably the only Japanese student studying at King Ed. Most of my friends were Chinese, and I still keep in touch with some of them. Because it was only recently that the Japanese have been allowed back to Vancouver, the Japanese population was very small and I had no contact with them.

After starting at King Ed, I realized I would need another year to complete senior matriculation before I could enter university to take architecture. Being impatient, I decided to take senior matriculation courses by correspondence while

46

still doing junior matriculation at King Edward High School; I would complete the missing subjects by attending summer school at the University of British Columbia, thereby saving one year. Not only was I able to accomplish all this, but I also got higher marks in math and physics on my senior matriculation examination than I did on my junior matriculation exam. When I decided to accelerate my studies, I could no longer carry out my work as a houseboy because I needed more time to study, so I left the household and stayed at a boarding house run by Mr. and Mrs. Popoff, who had by then moved to Vancouver.

After investigating where I should apply to take my architectural courses, I narrowed the choice down to the University of British Columbia, the University of Manitoba, and the University of Toronto. Although UBC was attractive for being closest to home, the faculty of architecture had started only recently, with most of the professors transferring from the University of Manitoba. I felt Toronto was too far away and did not have the same reputation as the University of Manitoba. So I chose the University of Manitoba.

5

University years

I spent five years, from September 1951 to May 1956, at the University of Manitoba, in Winnipeg, the capital city of Manitoba. It is situated in the geographical centre of Canada in the middle of the flat Canadian prairies where much of the wheat supply comes from. It has a typical continental climate—hot and dry in the summer and bitterly cold in the winter, especially with the wind-chill factor.

Lana, my wife, recalled an incident when she was in Winnipeg watching a film starring John Wayne, where he was stranded in some remote place shivering at how cold it was at minus 20 degrees Fahrenheit. The whole audience laughed out loud as it was minus 30 degrees Fahrenheit outside where they were. However cold the weather, I learned to appreciate the beauty of the winter season with the cold crisp air and the silence of the white environment, broken only by the sound of the frozen snow crunching under my feet. The people in Winnipeg are equipped to cope with the cold. The houses are well heated; there are heated shelters at every bus stop and electric plugs for the outdoor car parks. The people there are also very helpful. If your car is stranded, they will stop and ask if you need any help.

The faculty of architecture did not have a central building of it's own; instead, it was scattered in various "huts" tucked amongst the trees along the Red River. Consequently, we did a lot of walking to and from the classrooms to the studios, located in the huts, and back to our dormitories.

During my entire time at the university, I stayed at the university residence. It was one huge building, divided into men's and women's sections separated by a common dining hall. Each room had two beds, two desks and a walk-in closet space. I shared the room with several different people during my stay. The first year was with a French Canadian who later went to Ethiopia to teach. The other years, I shared the room with Tom Enta, a medical student from Toronto; unfortunately, he and I have lost contact now. Mealtime was flexible, but held within a certain given time span, so if I were to arrive late, some of the food would be finished. There was usually a lot of complaining from the students about the quality of the food, but I was quite satisfied.

The students were mainly from the Prairie Provinces, but there were an unusually high number of Chinese students from Hong Kong. Even today, a large number of Hong Kong students attend the University of Manitoba, contributing to the popularity of that university. Many of the members of the Canadian University Alumni Association in Hong Kong are from the University of Manitoba.

Professor John Russell was the Dean of the School of Architecture. He was a gentle, soft-spoken man, an excellent administrator, who was caring and dedicated but a poor teacher. He taught the course on colour, but his delivery made the lectures boring. He also taught Art History which was more interesting. He was well liked by the students and he genuinely cared for the school and the students. His brother-in-law, Professor Sellars, taught the course on building construction. The monotonous tone of his voice made his lectures so boring that they put us to sleep. Professor Dunkley, who taught the furniture course, was livelier, as was "Pinky," who taught Design Fundamentals and supervised the first year studio. Professor Donahue was always dressed in a very fashionable way with famous brand name clothes and boots. He also enjoyed his drinks. Professor Gerson was our supervisor in the senior design studios. He later transferred to the University of British Columbia, where my brother Gene went to study architecture. They were the permanent staff, but there were some younger men that came to supervise our design studios. The school also encouraged visiting architects to come and give talks to us. Buckminister Fuller was an outstanding speaker, so enthusiastic with his theories that he was able to inspire all of us.

Our class was one of the smallest compared with other years. This gave us a close comradeship and we tended to do things together. Bill Miske was the character of the class. I was amazed at how he could remember all the funny jokes, yet I could not understand why he did so badly in academic subjects. He was the

At the studio.

leader in our activities, especially when there were parties. John Phillips was the opposite—a quiet, serious and thin man. Harold Saxby hailed from Saskatoon, Al Burrows from Alberta and Alf Hennessey, who was colour blind, from Prince Edward Island. There was only one girl in our class, named Monika, who later married Roy Kiyooka, a Japanese Canadian artist.

In our third year, a new student appeared from Cambridge, England, since Cambridge did not grant architectural degrees. Geof Bargh was very intelligent and talented, the first to give me a real challenge at school. It was good for me, as I'd had it too easy before then. I understand that he is now teaching.

My best friends were Claude Deforest, who was a year ahead of me, and Stan Osaka, who was a year behind me. As Claude lived in Winnipeg, he invited me to his family's house very often, making me feel at home. I am very grateful for their warm hospitality. Claude's family was from Switzerland and they now make Canada their home. Claude was to eventually marry a Japanese girl, perhaps influenced by my being Japanese. He went on to teach at the university after working for Saarinen following his graduate studies at MIT. Stan Osaka came from Montreal, and when I visited Montreal during the school holidays, his family welcomed me. Together we would go out to activities organized by the Japanese community in Winnipeg, Toronto or Montreal, since we shared the same kinds of experiences during the war years.

The school offered a solid foundation for the study of architecture. One of the most interesting courses was the comprehensive course on the history of art, which covered the major stylistic periods in detail, from Egyptian and Babylonian through Greek, Roman, Romanesque, Gothic, Renaissance, the 17th and 18th centuries, and up to the modern period. Far Eastern art, however, was barely touched upon. We then went through the history of architecture, according to specific time periods; we also studied, in detail, the three masters: Mies van der Rohe, Frank Lloyd Wright and Le Corbusier. We became conscious of some other architects, such as Philip Johnson (a disciple of Mies), Alvar Aalto, Charles Eames, Oscar Niemeyer, Paul Rudolph, Louis Kahn, and Eero Saarinen. These men represented an exciting time for the flowering of architecture beyond the international style.

In my final year, I was elected Senior Stick, the head of the student body for the architecture and interior design faculty. This gave me some great responsibilities, such as looking after the welfare of the students, as well as organizing sports and social activities. Every year, the highlight of our social life was the Beaux Arts Ball. We all dressed up in costumes according to the theme chosen for that year. Some of the most imaginative and outrageous costumes were seen at that ball. One year, our class all went dressed as members of the Klu Klux Klan; the story appeared in the Winnipeg Press the following morning. Our costumes were timely as this was the era of racial troubles in Alabama.

My mother's younger sister, Fuji, and her family lived in Winnipeg. My uncle had an upholstering shop, for fixing old sofas and chairs. On weekends, I would go there to help out, learning how to lay the springs under the seats and helping with the delivery of those bulky sofas. After work, I would have a hearty Japanese or Chinese meal with rice, which I had missed very much. I was very happy to have a relative in Winnipeg to whom I could turn in any emergency. I also got to know the Japanese community in Winnipeg by going to some of their social functions. I got to meet Helen, a cousin of my roommate, Tom Enta, whom I took out to social functions. Her family was very kind to me and made my time in Winnipeg memorable.

In the evenings, I would go into town to the Winnipeg Art School to study drawing, painting and sculpture as extra subjects to further develop my skills. Harry Kiyooka, the younger brother of Roy Kiyooka, was studying art there. He encouraged me to try abstract art but I had to confess to him that I could not do abstract art because I didn't understand it. I had a very good teacher in sculpture and one of the pieces I did was a wood figure carrying a stone above his head (shown on page 48); the sculpture is still kept at the university. I thought it was a very good piece. I also learned how to work with clay to mould figures and busts, a skill that was to come in handy later in life.

During the years at the University of Manitoba, I was able to win many scholarships. The one that I really appreciated was the Isbister Scholarship, awarded in my first year, which gave me money to buy books. Without this prize, I could not have afforded to buy the expensive art and architectural books that I needed. In my gratitude for this award, I started a scholarship at the University of Hong Kong's Department of Architecture, called the J. H. Kinoshita Prize, which offers students an opportunity to obtain books. I always hope that the recipients appreciate it as much as I appreciated the Isbister Scholarship. I was able to finance myself through university with scholarships and summer jobs.

After completing the first year of university, the professors recommended that we gain practical experience by working in an architect's office. As Vancouver was the closest city to home, I first went there to look for a job. I tried every architect in Vancouver, but not one of them took me in. Most thought that I was too inexperienced to be of much use. It was true that I had no experience but I had to start somewhere. Feeling discouraged, I went home to Slocan and packed two suitcases. One was for city clothes, suitable for working in an architect's office. The second contained clothes for mining, as I had heard that the uranium mines in northern Saskatchewan were hiring and paying well. I told my parents that I was going to head eastward and try looking in every big city for a job in an architect's office, but if I failed, I would head north to the mines and send my office clothes home. They would then know which job I got by the content of the suitcase I sent back.

My first stop was Calgary, just on the other side of the Rockies. I was able to land a job with Rule, Wynn and Rule at my first interview; I sent the miner's clothes home. While there, I was able to enjoy the famous Calgary Stampede, which is held every summer for two weeks. The entire city joins in the celebration on the main street, which is closed to vehicle traffic for the occasion. Horses and people compete with each other for space. Competitions are held for bronco busting, lassoing, and other cowboy activities. Very little work gets done during these two weeks as most of the people are out in the street celebrating.

For two summers, I worked in Toronto with Page and Steele. I stayed with my uncle Sadao, the elder brother of my mother, in Toronto. They treated me like a member of the immediate family. My uncle loves to go fishing, so on weekends we would drive out to one of the many lakes near Toronto and go fishing for bass and pike. My second cousins, who were all living in Toronto, initiated me into the game of tennis. However, I could never hit the ball properly and, to this day, I remain a poor tennis player.

It was at Page and Steele, especially under Peter Dickenson, who was the chief designer, where I was to gain the most experience during my university years. Peter was not only a talented designer, but he also looked into problems very thoroughly. Once, he impressed me by setting up a full-scale outline of a window. He used strings to delineate the window and to show the size and position of both movable and fixed parts; this was to test whether the window could be cleaned from the inside by opening it. Even though I was just a summer student, he took the time and effort to guide me through design processes and details. He was an excellent teacher and my work experience at Page and Steele became a valuable part of my training. I firmly believe that summer training is a very important aspect of architectural education.

For most of the Christmas holidays, I would go home to Slocan and help my father at the store, which was very busy at the holiday season. During my second year at university, my father asked me to design a new store for him. Little did he realize how inexperienced a second-year student was, but I could not dis-

Slocan store, designed by JHK while in second year of architecture.

appoint him and, in my spare time, I designed the new store. It was a one-storey wood-frame structure with a pitched roof. It had a large glass wall facing the street and was solid on the other walls except for a few windows for daylight. It was modern in style—at least what I imagined to be modern at that time. I drew a perspective and showed it to my father, who liked it very much. Construction started that spring and was finished during the summer without any problems. My father had an experienced contractor who knew what he was doing, so he was able to interpret my drawings correctly even with inconsistencies. This was my first commission.

I finally graduated in May of 1956, winning the University Gold Medal for best student throughout the 5 years, and the RAIC (Royal Architectural Institute of Canada) Medal as the outstanding student in the graduating class of '56. I also won scholarships to Harvard and the Massachusetts Institute of Technology for graduate studies. I chose MIT because Dean Russell and Professor Sellers recommended it highly, as they were both MIT graduates. The Edward Langley Scholarship from AIA (America Institute of Architects), for $1,600, added to the financial help I received. I regret that I did not win the Pilkington Scholarship, which is for the best thesis of the graduating year. This award went to Geof Bargh.

Aug 15/56
Angeleri Cafe
Vancouver.
Cena

6

Lana Cheung

Pow! A snowball hit the window next to my drafting desk while I was preparing my thesis. I looked out and saw a Chinese girl smiling and waving at me. My heart skipped. This was to be the beginning of a romance that eventually led to marriage.

Lana Cheung was one of the many Chinese students from Hong Kong who were studying at University of Manitoba. She was taller than the average Chinese girl with an attractive long oval face and long black hair. She was taking Interior Design, which was in the same faculty as architecture, so we shared a lot of lectures. The design studio was housed in a hut next to ours. Both the interior design and architectural students were required to do their theses in the last term of the final year. It was a time of intensive work, and in the final month before the deadline, we were working almost 20 hours every day, with hardly any sleep. It must be human nature to do as much as possible within the given deadline, even though we could have opted out by not working so hard. It was during this period that the snowball incident occurred and led to our helping each other with our respective theses.

Lana's thesis was on a Chinese Embassy in Canada, and it had some Chinese characters on the drawings. I was helping her to stick some of these characters on the presentation board, but being unfamiliar with Chinese characters, I put them on upside down! After so many sleepless nights, I was very tired and I guess my brain was not very alert. Or was it the state of my mind? One evening near midnight, when I was working on my drafting board, Lana brought me a hot bowl of fried rice, which I really appreciated. I naturally thought that she had made it herself, but I discovered many years later that she had just warmed up a bowl of *chow fan* that her friend had brought back from Chinatown. That put to rest any notions about the power of her cooking, but it's the thought that counts, I always say to myself.

Lana Yuen Shiu Cheung was born in Hong Kong, when her family was living in Glenealy Street, just above the central business district, commonly referred to as "Central." Later they moved to Kowloon Tong where she grew up. Kowloon Tong was not developed at that time and was almost rural in character. She was the youngest of six children. Her eldest brother is Peter, followed by sisters Madeline and Gladys, brother Johnny, sister Rita and then herself. Being the youngest in the family, she was mostly in the care of her amah and learned to be independent.

In 1941, her father saw some low-flying planes above their house. He thought it was the British Air Force just practicing, until he saw them dropping bombs. Hong Kong was being attacked.

There was panic everywhere. Lana was taught that the safest place to be during a bombing is under a table, so she squatted under the table until the bombardment ended. However, it was not safe to live in an isolated house, because of gangs roaming around, looting and stealing. The family evacuated to the home of friends, the Fu family, who lived on Tak Shing Street, in Kowloon, and had a guard watching over the compound. (The Fus were an old family from Macao whose eldest son married Lana's eldest sister a short time later.)

When the Cheung family was packing to move, it was chaos. Lana's mother forgot to pack her precious jewellery and cash and instead packed all her cosmetics. Lana got a large *On Lok Yuen* can and stuffed it full of biscuits.

After the surrender of Hong Kong, their house was occupied by a Japanese officer who was the head of artillery. He asked the servants who were left behind in the house why their master did not stay in the house. They replied that it was because they were afraid. The officer told them not to be afraid and encouraged everyone to return to their home. Lana and her brother Johnny moved back to Kowloon Tong. Lana remembers the officer as being old, tall and skinny, and he was very kind to her, allowing her to go into his room, which had a huge map pinned to the wall. (Too bad she was not a spy.) One day, he gave Lana a puppy, but Lana declined saying she didn't have enough food to feed the dog. So the officer started to give her rice and canned corned beef, which she used to feed herself, while giving the leftovers to the puppy.

After a while, the family decided to move to Macao, a neutral territory, where they had a family house. They all crammed inside this large three-storey house on a shady tree-lined boulevard facing the sea. Her mother raised cash for food by selling her jewellery, which she had kept in a safety deposit box. Later, the ground floor was rented out to the British Consulate, while they lived on the upper floors, and they used the rental income to keep going. This house is still standing there, and is now used as a school, but it is no longer located on the seashore but is far inland—the result of land reclamation.

Lana received her education in the Chinese stream. After the war she went to Pui Ching School, as it was close to her home in Kowloon Tong. After she finished middle school at Pui Ching, they did not accept any girls for high school education, so she instead had to go to Ling Nam in Canton. At Pui Ching, she established a lot of close and deep friendships with her classmates. This class was very strong and active and, to this day, there are many reunions and other social activities. In 2001, we attended the 50th anniversary of their class at Canton, where many alumni members gathered from the United States, Canada, Australia, Macao, and from all over China, with the biggest group coming from Hong Kong.

After Pui Ching, Lana went to Royden House for two years where she mixed with the students from Shanghai who were escaping from the Communist takeover of China. Her classmates included sons and daughters of very prominent figures who had to flee China: Roger, son of Big-eared Tu of the notorious Green Gang; Sonny Lim, whose father was number two in the air force; George Tso, son of the contractor Paul Y Tso; and Janet Chau, whose father was also a prominent figure in the air force.

Lana did well at Royden House, becoming a prefect even though she was not a senior. She has many pleasant memories of her life there. At Royden House, she won a prize of $100, which she used to pay for registration at Ling Nam University in Canton. She did not tell her father that she wanted to go to Ling Nam University until after she was accepted.

Lana excelled at school and often found herself to be the youngest in her class, as many of the other students had lost time during the disruption of the war years. She was often teased for being the teacher's pet, since most of the teachers responded to her in a favourable way. She was also very active in sports, winning races, high jump, and other school sports. However, pictures of her youth show her to be a glamour girl, with shapely legs. She was actually named Lucy when she was born, but her friends changed it to Lana, after the movie actress Lana Turner.

Her close friends in Hong Kong were Brenda ("Dum Dum") and Anna

Sun. Brenda was her cousin and sporty like Lana. They would often challenge each other as to who could first run and climb up to Lion's Rock, which was located just behind their home. They would bicycle to Star Ferry for their favourite treat, an ice cream cone. They have remained very close, even to this day, though Brenda now lives in Oakland. Anna Sun, her classmate for many years, was the grand niece of Dr. Sun Yat Sen, the founder of modern China.

After the communists took over China, Lana studied at Ling Nam University in Canton and contemplated joining the Red Guards to help build up China. Her father became alarmed at this and asked her to return to Hong Kong. She discussed where to continue her studies with her father. He discouraged her going

1953 – Lana at the University of Manitoba.

to America because he felt their society was too loose and would not be good for a single young girl. So she investigated Canada instead and was encouraged to go to the University of Manitoba by many of her friends who were already studying there. Lana was accepted and took the ocean liner, the *Queen Mary*, to San Francisco.

Later, a senior student at the University of Manitoba met her and helped her to orient herself to Canada and to university life. She lived at the university residence in the women's wing, so I was often able to see her in the dining room and also at the classes we shared. Lana always sat in the front row in class, giving her full attention to the lecture.

On one occasion, she was to beat me. It was in the colour class given by Professor Dunklee. We were presented with a whole row of coloured chips and we had to rearrange them in the right order of value within a given time limit. Lana got a perfect score and I came second with one mistake. She once entered a poster competition for the Royal Winnipeg Ballet. She designed a poster in bold graphics and colours advertising "The Royal Winnipeg Ballet 1954." For this

1954 – Left to right: Carol, Joanna, Gerry, Babs and Lana.

she won two tickets to the ballet, a real treat since she could not afford the price of a ticket. On another occasion, when she was making a costume for the ball held at the residence, Miss Harland, the head of Interior Design, asked what she was making. She replied that she was making a tube of Colgate toothpaste. Miss Harland looked very serious and told her in a stern voice not to be squeezed by the boys. For this she won the most original costume. She was an outstanding student and won many scholarships, such as the University Bronze Medal and the Thesis Prize when she graduated.

During the university years, she had a boyfriend from Hong Kong, named Stephen Wong, but after a year at the University of Manitoba, he transferred to Dalhousie University, so she was only able to see him during the summer months. When she sported a diamond ring, everybody thought that she was engaged to Stephen—Stephen had a group of loyal friends at the University of Manitoba who took Lana out as part of the gang. I thought that she was unavailable, which was reinforced when I asked her out for a dance at the residence and was refused. Lana later explained to me that a girl would never accept such an invitation if given on the same day as the dance. It would be an insult to the girl. I never thought of it that way—I had left it until the last minute because I was afraid to ask.

Lana always had to work during the summer holidays. Her allowance from her parents covered only the school term, so for the summer holidays, she had to earn her own way. The first summer, she went to Banff to look for work. She wasn't able to get a job in the prestigious Banff Hotel as a chambermaid because she did not have any experience making beds. So she ended up working in a Chinese restaurant as a cashier, as she was better at numbers than at serving. On her days off, she would help a local rancher lead his row of tourists on a horseback ride through the Rocky Mountains. She had learned to ride as a child, encouraged by her father, who was an Anglophile, but she was actually afraid of horses. However, these horses were very tame and knew far better than the riders where to go. They were certainly eager to get home after doing their rounds. During Christmas holidays she would work as a gift-wrapper at the Hudson's Bay department store.

Today, our children are very fortunate to be able to come home from their studies in the UK or America during the summer holidays as well as the Christmas holidays. Lana was not able to go home or to see her parents until she had finished her four years at the university and completed her one-year professional training in Canada.

Lana and JHK in 1956.

7

MIT and beyond

I did not stay for the graduation ceremony at the University of Manitoba, as I had a summer job waiting for me in Vancouver with the planning division of the Kitimat Corporation. They were the company that oversaw the production of aluminium. The town of Kitimat was located far to the north of Vancouver, on the coast of British Columbia. It was one of the great engineering feats of that time. Aluminium production requires a great deal of electricity. Hydroelectric power was harnessed by damming a river on the east side of the coastal range of British Columbia, creating a lake, and then tunnelling westward through the mountains to a turbine located on the coast. The alumina ore was brought by sea from South America to Kitimat and was processed by smelting it into aluminium, using hydroelectric power. As Kitimat was a new town, everything had to be planned from scratch and I was to be part of that team. I was to use Kitimat as the basis of my thesis at MIT the following year.

My brother Gene and I rented an apartment in Kitsilano for the summer. Gene was studying architecture at the University of British Columbia and took a summer job in Vancouver. We fixed up the apartment with our own money, improving the premises so much that the landlord reduced our rent for the final month. Lana Cheung also worked in Vancouver to gain her work experience. This was not deliberately planned; we both had gotten our jobs in Vancouver quite independently. She worked for Wilson Stationery, which provided office planning as one of their services to customers buying their office furniture there. She was living at the YWCA, which was located in the centre of town. Although it was convenient, the disadvantage was that there was a curfew, after which time the front door would be locked.

We often went out to our favourite restaurant, Scott's on Granville Street, which served delicious fried clams. (We returned many years later to find, to our great disappointment, that the restaurant has disappeared.) One Saturday evening, Lana and I, with Gene and his girlfriend, a very attractive Japanese girl, went up the chairlift to the top of Grouse Mountain to have dinner at a special restaurant overlooking the spectacular view of Vancouver. However, when we got off the chairlift at the top of the mountain, there were still patches of snow along the path leading to the restaurant. Being gallant, I swooped Lana up and carried her across the snow patch to dry land. Gene followed my actions but slipped and fell, dropping the poor girl and leaving her sprawled all over the snow. It looked so hilarious that I started to laugh out loud, causing great embarrassment to my brother. Later, Lana was to reproach me for my insensitive action.

I figured that this girl was good for me. One long weekend, I took her home to Slocan to meet my parents, where she was a hit. I showed her all the places that were precious in my youth—the creek where we went fishing, the trail where we hiked, the place where we picked berries, and the school I had attended. Lana had a friend from Hong Kong who was once her roommate at the University of Manitoba and who had also spent the same summer in Vancouver. Her name was Eleanor Kwong and we went out with her on many occasions. She is now living in Vancouver, and is married to Ken Lee, my classmate from the King Edward days.

Summer was soon to end and I had to go to Boston to take my postgraduate studies at MIT. Lana stayed behind in Vancouver to fulfill her professional requirements before returning to Hong Kong. When I left for Boston, I promised Lana that I would go to Hong Kong and ask for her hand in marriage. With that promise, I was able to face the future with a purpose.

I felt very lonely at MIT. After a wonderful summer with Lana, I was now alone in a strange city trying to find my bearings. As there were no campus accommodations for graduate students, except for married students, I spent the first few nights camped in the basement of one of the buildings at MIT with hundreds of other students. By looking at notices, I was able to find a room in a house across the Charles River on Beacon Street. There were no cooking facilities in the room, so I had to eat out, which did not help my limited finances. Every day, I walked across the Massachusetts Avenue Bridge to MIT. In the winter, when the icy winds blew across the bridge, it was bitterly cold. My memories of MIT are not happy ones.

The scholarships and my summer work were enough to see me financially through MIT. The tuition was $1,100 USD per year, which sounds so reasonable now compared to $30,000 USD today. The Edward Langley Scholarship was worth $1,600 USD and, with the scholarship from MIT for tuition for the first term, I had enough for both my lodgings and my living expenses. Like many students, I worked part time to help with my expenses; I worked for a local architect, named Samuel Glazer, who was known for hiring students from MIT.

The Dean of the Faculty was Professor Pietro Belluschi, a well-known architect from the northwest. However, we did not see much of him, for he was too busy. The person who actually taught us was Professor Anderson, who was

Stadium Project - influenced by Catalano.

to become the dean soon after Belluschi. Professor Catalano, who came from Argentina, taught the design class. He influenced me a great deal as I developed my direction in architecture. He emphasized that architectural form must integrate with a clear structural logic that is both efficient and economical. From this principle, the artistic integration of structure and architecture will follow.

A visiting speaker, Professor Rudolfski, was to shatter the foundation of my training with his lecture on "Architecture without Architects." He demonstrated that architects are not necessary in order to produce good architecture. He illustrated this with examples of indigenous shelters in Africa, Asia and Europe, such as the circular "Arabello" dwellings in southern Italy. He made us wonder why we were studying architecture.

The students were the heart of the school. They came from all over the world, from different backgrounds and training, which made the environment stimulating and exciting. There was Pierre Cabrol and Jacques from Beaux Arts in Paris, Naibu Akashi from Waseda in Tokyo, Chong Keat Lim from Singapore, John Morphett from Australia, Holtzbauer from Germany, David Gosling from

70

Entry for the Enrico Fermi Competition; co-designed with Naebu Akashi.

the UK and Don Hansen and Earl Flansburgh, among others, from the United States. Somehow the Asian students tended to get together; it may be the craving for rice that holds us closer, I don't know. Chong Keat Lim, Naibu and I would get together frequently to go to Chinatown for Chinese food. A friend of Chong Keat, Ronald Brunskill, from the University of Manchester, was attending MIT on a research scholarship, so he would also join us for a Chinese meal or for a concert at the Boston Symphony.

We were given several group projects to work on together as well as some individual projects. Naibu Akashi and I teamed up for a competition to commemorate Enrico Fermi, the 1938 Nobel Prize winner in physics, who was known as "the father of the atomic bomb." We worked hard on it, but it did not win for its architecture, which we had concentrated on, but for its brilliant concept. The winning entry had a series of huge organ pipes sticking out of an open plaza with all the facilities tucked under the plaza. It was music that was to hold the memory of Fermi.

For my thesis, I chose a project in Kitimat, which I was able to research during my summer work. When I presented my thesis, the jury judged that it was not well enough developed, so I had to stay during the summer holidays to develop it further. I finally graduated in September.

That winter, before Christmas, Lana was coming out to New York to join her brother, John and sisters Madeline, Gladys and Rita to sail on the Queen Elizabeth to visit Europe on her way home. I went to New York to meet her before she boarded the ship. When I met her eldest sister, Madeline, I asked if I could talk to her privately, but she shied away, not wanting to act on behalf of her parents if I asked for Lana's hand. I was able to meet not only her family, but also many of her friends who saw her off at the pier.

Lana sailed to the UK and then traveled through Europe to end up in Milan. It was just before Christmas and Milan would be dead for tourism, so they decided instead to go to Cortina d'Ampezzo to spend Christmas. They took the train and when they arrived at Cortina, all the hotels were full and they couldn't get a single room. Discouraged, they dragged their luggage back to the train station where they met a kindly priest who asked them where they were they going. They replied that they couldn't find any rooms in Cortina so they were planning to go back to Milan. The priest immediately made a phone call and got them rooms in the most prestigious hotel in Cortina, located above the village on the ski slope. So it was in Cortina that Lana first learned how to ski. Lana was very impressed with the young men in Italy as they were very courteous, thoughtful, and considerate—characteristics that Lana claims I do not possess.

After graduating from MIT, I wanted to gain experience and earn enough to go to Hong Kong so I decided to head westward by Greyhound. My first stop was in Detroit, Michigan. I went to Sarinin's office to find work since my friend, Claude de Forest, was working there after completing MIT a year ahead of me. There were no openings, however, so I tried Minoru Yamasaki, later of World Trade Centre fame, but also no luck. So I continued on my way west, but since

I wanted to see New Orleans, I took a southern detour to get there. From there, I took the train to Los Angeles, where I was able to get a job in the planning department of an architectural and planning firm called Pereira and Luckman.

The pay was not very good, but I was desperate for a job, so I took it. I was able to find a small unit below a garage in the Hollywood Hills, which was close to the office on Sunset Boulevard. A car is a necessity in California, so I acquired my first car, a second or third hand Studebaker. I put a lot of mileage onto that car, using it to explore areas far from Los Angeles, such as the Grand Canyon, Monument Valley, Mesa Verde, Bryce Canyon, and places closer to Los Angeles, such as Santa Barbara, San Diego and San Francisco. I made many of these trips with Pierre Cabrol, from MIT, who had found a job with Welton Beckett. We also went across the border to Tijuana, Mexico, to see an occasional bullfight.

The partnership of Pereira and Luckman was breaking up and many of the staff were taking sides and creating an antagonistic atmosphere. At this time, I got a call from Dave Lepore, who used to work for Sam Glazer in Boston and was now working for Sheraton Corporation, to tell me that they were creating a new architectural department to handle new projects and they needed designers. He asked if I would like to join them. I agreed and, after a year in Los Angeles, I again packed my clothes and headed back to Boston where I was to stay for another two years.

The work at Sheraton taught me how a hotel is put together, a lesson that was to serve me well when I arrived in Hong Kong. The headquarters of Sheraton, which was located in Boston, had a special department for each area of hotel operations. If a client wanted Sheraton to manage a hotel in a foreign country, I would first get together with the marketing staff who would conduct a study on the requirements of the proposed hotel, such as the number of rooms, size of the rooms, the number and types of restaurants, the size of ballroom, if required, etcetera. I would then send the client the result of this market survey together with the standards of Sheraton—typical layout and size of bedrooms, size of beds, layout and size of bathrooms, corridor width and service areas, such as the kitchens and other back-of-the-house requirements. After the local architect designed the hotel according to our guidelines, he would send the preliminary plans to us for comments. I would then consult and coordinate with various departments, such as front desk, housekeeping, personnel, food and beverage, and engineering, to make sure that the size, layout and relationship of each space was correct.

Sometimes, if the architect was not familiar with designing a hotel, he would come to Boston and we would work together to design the hotel. The hotel in Tel Aviv is an example of this arrangement. I would do all the preliminary designs for the hotels that were owned by Sheraton, mainly the ones in Hawaii; I particularly enjoyed these projects, as I was given a free hand to be creative. The architectural department was fairly new in the organization, so my arrival was very timely. The head of the architectural department was Mary Kennedy, an interior designer who rose up in the organization by doing renovation work for the hotel through the interior design department, which was a large group in the organization,

I enjoyed that stay in Boston much better than when I was a poor student at MIT. I had a large upstairs room in an apartment owned by a spinster, who was very careful about the company I could invite to my room. Later, I shared a house in Sommerville with Paul Shimamoto, an MIT graduate from Hawaii who worked for Catalano, my professor at MIT. Paul had a car, and every weekend in the winter, we would go skiing in New Hampshire or Vermont. Paul was a fantastic cook so we ate well, but I always ended up doing the dishes.

8

Architecture and nature in Japan

After two years of working for Sheraton, I had enough money saved to go to Hong Kong. As Hong Kong is halfway around the world, I planned the trip to take the opportunity to see both Japan and Europe, as every architect dreams of doing. My first stop would be Japan for two months to see the latest, as well as the traditional, forms of architecture there. The next stop would be Hong Kong to ask for Lana's hand in marriage. We would then spend our honeymoon in Europe.

My brother Gene planned to join us in Europe, as he had just graduated from his postgraduate studies in architecture at Yale and was just as anxious as I was to see the architectural wonders of Europe. I ordered a car, a French Simca, to be picked up in Europe. It was my plan that we could combine our honeymoon with a grand architectural tour of Europe, killing two birds with one stone. I also planned that after our honeymoon in Europe, we would come back to Boston and I would continue with my work with the Sheraton Corporation. Mrs. Kennedy had already arranged for my leave of absence and kept my position free. But as things later turned out, certain of these plans would end up being changed. My trip to Japan, however, went much as I had intended.

Before I started on my trip, I spent Christmas with my parents in Slocan and explained my future plans to them. They gave me their full support, and my parents' friends made contributions to my coming trip and wished me well.

I arrived in Tokyo on January 3, 1960, in the middle of winter. I immediately called on Stan Osaka, a schoolmate at the University of Manitoba, who was then living in Japan. This was the second time I had been to Japan, but I had been too young to remember much on my first trip. Stan introduced me to the sights and sounds of Tokyo. I was pleasantly surprised that my Japanese was just adequate enough to be able to get around Japan.

My first duty was to see my relatives, some of whom I had never met before. I took a train to Hikone to see my grandfather and grandmother, who were now living with my mother's youngest sister, Tomi, and her second husband. Aunt Tomi had a sad past. Her first husband was killed during the war and her only son drowned while fishing with my grandfather. While grandfather was rowing the boat, he suddenly noticed that the boy, who was sitting behind him, had disappeared. By the time he realized the boy was gone, it was too late, and he had already drowned.

My grandfather's house was a large two-storey building made of wood with a pitched roof in a traditional Japanese style. It had a western-style living room as well as a Japanese-style living room. On either side of the house was a Japanese style garden with several stone lanterns. It was considered to be one of the grandest houses in Hikone, although it was dark and gloomy inside; perhaps it was the winter condition that emphasized this depressing impression. I never felt happy or cheerful in this house—bad *feng shui*, as the Chinese would say.

My father's younger sister Hisako lived nearby in Kawachi, with her par-

Grandmother and Grandfather
Maikawa, 1960.

ents-in-law and her family. They were a very warm family and my visit was cheerful and happy. I also went to visit my new relative Osamu Kinoshita—formerly a
Yamamoto—at our house in Kawaminami, quite close to Hikone. He was kind
enough to take me to Nara on my first visit there. I was to return to Nara several
times to see in-depth what I had missed before.

My grandfather took me to Taga San, a shrine near Hikone. At the
shrine, Grandfather prayed and tried his luck at one of the fortune boxes, where
one shakes a container until a stick drops out; just for the fun of it, I tried it too.
However, grandfather wouldn't read his slip of paper—or perhaps he didn't like
what he saw and didn't want to reveal it—and I couldn't read mine because I

cannot read Japanese characters, so we both put our papers in our pockets and went home. On another occasion, he took me to Hikone Castle where we had a good view of Lake Biwa. From there, we descended, in the snow, to take a walk through the Raku Raku Koen, or garden, at the base of the castle.

The main purpose of my trip to Japan was to study the architecture, both ancient and modern. I was a great admirer of Kenzo Tange, a modern architect, who created a new vocabulary with a distinct Japanese flavour for modern buildings. I traveled all over Japan to see his work, especially in the south of Tokyo. The first thing I did when I got to Japan was to meet Tange. He was a small thin man with thick straight hair, which was pulled back. He was soft spoken and kind, and was generous in receiving me, a young, unknown and inexperienced

JHK with Grandfather Maikawa.

78

recent graduate.

He took me around his office and showed me the drawings and early sketch models of the National Gymnasium, which would become one of his best works. From his office, I got the list of buildings he had completed and I planned my travels in Japan based on this list; most of Tange's pre-1960 work was done outside of Tokyo. It was just about at this time that he became famous internationally and was starting to get commissions in Tokyo. The only building Tange had completed in Tokyo was the Tokyo Metropolitan Government Offices, which were modern looking with very fine detailing. The American Express office in Tokyo became my base of operations; here I collected my mail and made flight reservations.

I next went to Kyoto, which is only an hour's train ride from Hikone, to study traditional Japanese architecture. Kyoto is my favourite city in Japan. It has the flavour of old Japan with its low wooden buildings, narrow streets and wealth of traditional architecture. I visited most of the temples and shrines in Kyoto, and the one that I enjoyed the most was Katsura Rikyu, the imperial villa and its garden. The way in which the buildings blend and merge with the landscape is carried out in a natural and gentle fashion. The buildings are skilfully situated to become part of the landscape. The landscape itself is probably the best I have seen. At the famed sand Zen garden at Ryoanji, I was surprised to see that the scale was much smaller than I had anticipated. In the photographs, there is no scale so I had imagined this garden would be much larger than was the actual reality. Later, as I went back again and again, I was able to capture the essence of the careful placement of the rocks in the sand and increase my appreciation of it.

A second trip to Nara to see Horyuji Temple was a must. It was built in the seventh century following the architecture of the Tang dynasty in China, and is considered to be one of the oldest surviving wooden buildings in the world. Unfortunately, almost all of the Tang dynasty buildings in China, with the exception of Nanchan Si and Foguang Si at Wutaishan, were destroyed due to Buddhist persecution or civil war, leaving only Japan to preserve these superb examples of Tang architecture.

From Kyoto, I headed to Hiroshima to see the Peace Centre, completed in 1955 by Tange to commemorate the atomic bombing of Hiroshima in 1945. The main building used a finely finished off-form concrete and pilotis, or supports, reminiscent of Corbusier. The bridge leading to the main building has a concrete railing that is shaped like a piece of sculpture. The exhibition inside the Centre, along with the bombed-out shell of a building they keep as a memorial, are a silent testimony to the horrors of war and, in particular, to the terrible impact of powerful bombs such as the atomic and hydrogen bombs.

From Kyoto, I made a side trip to Miyajima where the main attraction is the Itsukushima Shrine with its familiar vermilion *torii*, or gate, floating in the water, as featured in every Japan travel brochure I have seen. I came to satisfy my curiosity as to why this location is considered to be one of the three most scenic views in Japan. I expected to be disappointed in it as a tourist destination, but I was proven wrong. It is a wonderful tourist destination; the setting is truly enchanting and it deserves its reputation. I got up very early next morning to see the building in early morning mist. As the sky became light, and the mist lifted, the vermilion *torii* emerged from the silent sea like a ghost. Then the shrine, which projects onto the water, started to emerge out of the mist to complete the image. Soon the mountain behind the shrine unfolded to form a dark background to the vermilion shrine and the *torii* floating on the water. I was overwhelmed by the scene; it was truly magical.

The shrine is situated over the water in a small bay at the base of a heavily forested mountain with the *torii* located on the central axis of the shrine at the mouth of the bay. The *torii* set into the sea symbolizes that the whole island is sacred. No one is permitted to give birth or die on the island, so there are no maternity wards or cemeteries. No trees are allowed to be cut, so the forest is still virgin and green. The way in which the building and the *torii* relate to the surrounding nature and to the sea is so sensitive and balanced that it made a deep impression upon me. It made me appreciate the great importance of the relationship that architecture and nature have with each other. This was the greatest lesson that my trip to Japan had taught me.

Nagasaki was the second city that was hit by an atomic bomb. However, there was little evidence of this tragedy. Although noted as the city where the Japanese were to first encounter the Portuguese and the Dutch in 1571, there was very little evidence of this part of the history. There were no noted historical or modern buildings, so I proceeded to Kumamoto to see Kumamoto Castle, one of the great fortresses of Japan. I took a ferry to Matsuyama in Shikoku, one of the other major islands.

In Matsuyama, I visited Tange's Ehime Civic Hall, which is a shallow dome enclosing a large auditorium. Then I carried on to Imabari to visit Tange's Imabari City and Public Hall. This building was also reminiscent of Corbusier, with its off-form concrete. I then went across the island to Takamatsu City to visit Tange's Kagawa Prefectural Government Offices. This concrete building has balconies all around the external walls, giving it a pagoda-like feeling.

I also visited the Ritsurin Park, one of the famous gardens in Japan built by the Matsudaira family. I crossed the inland sea by ferry from Takamatsu to Okayama, taking third class to save money. The sea was extremely rough; everybody in the hold of third class was getting sick and, just smelling the foul air, I felt like vomiting. To escape, I went up to the deck, but it was windy and very cold. Instead, I went inside at the deck level, which I later discovered was the first-class lounge. Fortunately, everybody was in their cabins so I was all alone to enjoy the luxurious space, and nobody came to check my ticket.

At Okayama, I visited the famed Koraku-en Garden, one of Japan's three famous gardens. Unlike the usual small gardens of Japan, this garden is open with a large expanse of lawn. Near Okayama was Kurashiki, an interesting town where many of the traditional storehouses or granaries (*kura*) are preserved, to create a distinct character in the heart of the old city. I saw many beautiful items, such as straw raincoats (no longer in use), displayed at the folk art museum. Before returning to Hikone, I visited Hemeji, where I saw the grandest of Japan's castles.

Looking back at the works of Tange, I believe it is evident that his earlier works were only experiments at blending Japanese characteristics into modern buildings. He used concrete as his medium and was influenced by Corbusier in buildings such as his Public Hall in Imabari and the Old Kurashiki City Hall. He also introduced elements of Japanese character, such as external railings on balconies, at Kagawa Prefectural Government Offices, or the railings of the bridge at the Hiroshima Peace Centre.

I feel that his highest achievement was in integrating a Japanese feeling into a modern form as he did with the National Gymnasium. I was fortunate to see it both while under design development in his office, in 1960, and at completion, in 1964. The bold statement made by the massive sweeping roof echoes the imposing roof of the Kyoto Imperial Palace—with its distinctive crown made by a heavy ridge piece, also reminiscent of the Shinto shrines of Ise or Izumo—and with the upturned ends on the ridge, Tange's building also recalls the Toshodaiji, or Todaiji, in Nara, which is derived from Tang architecture.

9

Making Hong Kong my home

I arrived in Hong Kong at 8:00 a.m. on March 3, 1960. It was my first trip to Hong Kong and little did I realize that it would become my permanent home. As the plane landed, I saw Lana from a distance. I could recognize her by her clothes and her pose. I did not feel excited or emotional; it felt as though we had been apart for only a few days. After the customs formality, I met her and our hands joined. I felt very happy. We had lunch together at the Gloucester Hotel with her father. My first impression of him was that of an English gentleman—polite, well-mannered and immaculately dressed. That evening, I had dinner at Lana's home and met her mother who looked at me carefully but did not say much.

My first impression of Hong Kong was that it was similar to Japan. The faces were similar, and the crowded streets were full of people with black hair. Hong Kong was still a city of low-rise buildings, with a great deal of colonial character. Along the waterfront, across from the Star Ferry, were located the old Prince's building, the old Post Office building, the former Queen's building where the Mandarin Hotel now stands, with covered colonnades on the street level to give protection from the frequent heavy rains.

The only large and substantial buildings were the Hong Kong and Shang-hai Bank buildings, the Bank of China, Alexandra House and the Peninsula Hotel across the harbour. The waterfront was where Connaught Road now runs. Rickshaws still roamed the streets. This charming colonial character was soon to be shattered with new buildings springing up all over Central; I was to be partly responsible for some of these. Looking back, I miss the old colonial character of Hong Kong, but I find it difficult to see how this character could have been kept with the force of such relentless development.

Lana and I had been apart for three years, and through these years, our passionate correspondence had become less frequent. When I saw Lana again, the dormant feelings were revived, but we had to get to know each other again. Twelve days after my arrival, I asked for her hand. She did not wish to rush into marriage, nor was she ready to take a honeymoon trip to Europe, followed by a move to North America. She was not keen to leave Hong Kong as she had now established herself, and she also felt we needed time to get to know each other again.

She told me to go ahead and join my brother Gene in Europe, as I had planned, and to come back later. But I felt that this would mean the end of our relationship, so I decided to stay. I wrote to Gene that I could not join him in Europe and that he would have to take the trip by himself.

I took a room with an English family who lived in the same block as Lana's family. Now the situation was completely different from the time we were at the university. Here, she had her family, relatives and friends, whereas I did not know a soul. I was completely dependent on her. Lana and her family were wonderful to me and very helpful in making me feel at home. In some respects, I noticed that Lana had changed—she was more realistic, although she remained a roman-tic and still is, even to this day. Some days when I was alone, I would wonder whether I was doing the right thing, but as soon as I saw her, my feelings would drown any doubts.

Lana was working for a decorating company called Peck and Wilson, which was owned by Joseph Li Fook Pui, a friend of hers. Her job was to design the premises that Peck and Wilson were commissioned to do. Her projects at that time were Andrew Eu's apartment and office, T. Y. Wong's office, Y. C. Wong's house, and renovations to the Miramar Hotel. Lana had been working for Peck and Wilson for two years and had made a name for herself as a talented interior designer. Soon after I arrived, she started her own firm, Lana Cheung, BID, AIID, first located in the old Alexandra House in Central. In those early days, I used to go and help her do some of the drafting. Even after I got a job with

JAL office interior, designed by Lana.

Palmer and Turner, I helped her in the evenings when there was an urgent need to complete the work. Later, before our first child was born, she moved to the garage space of her parent's home on College Street. It was two storeys high, so she created a cockloft for additional space and installed a glass front to the garage, which made it look like an office space.

Lana had enjoyed herself tremendously since her return to Hong Kong, and recalls it as the best time of her life. While carefree and single, she was very popular at social functions and there were many suitors who chased after her, but she was enjoying herself too much to take them seriously. My arrival must have upset her way of life, as she had to "take care" of me, since I was a stranger to the city. I attended various social events, while I was there. I was invited to the Hawaiian Night at the old Foreign Correspondence Club by Billy Poy, a popular man about town, whose daughter, Adrienne Clarkson, later became the Governor General of Canada. His daughter-in-law, Vivienne (daughter of Dick Lee of the Lee Hysan family), is a senator in the Canadian government as well as the chancellor of the University of Toronto.

The late Andrew Eu invited me to a private dinner at Eucliffe. Andrew and I were later to be baptized together in preparation for our future weddings. Andrew Eu's fianceé, Sandra, was a beauty queen from Hawaii. Lana was Andrew's godmother for the baptism. After our wedding, I asked my mother whether I was ever baptized and she replied, of course I was, so it ended up that I had been baptized twice.

During weekends, we would explore the New Territories, visiting old village temples and houses. At that time, the old villages were fairly intact without the intrusions of the modern three-storey Spanish style houses that are so prevalent today. We would often end up at Lana's parents' retreat in Ting Kau, where they owned some rental houses. There was a pavilion at the top of the hill with a swimming pool, fed by a fresh water stream. It was truly idyllic to relax in this

Hawaiian Night. From left to right: JHK, Lana, Lana's parents and Billy Poy.

haven away from urban life. Here, her parents entertained their numerous friends for Sunday lunches.

One of the activities that Lana excelled in was water skiing. She had taken it up after she had returned to Hong Kong and found that she was a natural-born skier. She got up on double skis the first time, and the next day she was on single skis. She would quit work early or go on weekends, joining her boss, Joseph Li, when he took five people out on his powerful speedboat. They would single ski all the way from Deep Water Bay to Ting Kau. After I arrived, I was invited to participate. I wasn't as flexible as Lana and needed three attempts before I could master single skis. One day in Ting Kau, I landed right on top of a huge jellyfish. I had red slashes all over my back, as though I had been whipped, and that night I developed a high fever in spite of the ammonia that was applied to my wounds. After that incident, I much preferred snow skiing.

Aside from water skiing, we often went on launch picnics with friends. Sailing out for a couple of hours to a secluded cove, isolated from civilization, was the perfect escape from the urban life of Hong Kong. Now, with the increase of

Lana waterskiing.

cruisers and launches, these coves are not so secluded and one will invariably have neighbours. After swimming in the clear water and water skiing, we would return to the harbour at twilight, while the glittering lights of Hong Kong imparted a sense of magic.

Lana's father, Andrew Yau Kuen Cheung, was the only son of the fourth concubine of her grandfather, Cheung Sik Hin. Her grandmother had married Cheung Sik Hin when she was quite young, and he already had grownup children from other wives; this created a situation familiar in many Chinese families: a niece or a nephew could be older than an aunt or uncle. C. K. Cheung, one of Lana's nephews, and an accomplished architect, had to call her "Auntie," in spite of being older. The Cheung family is one of the old Cantonese families of Hong Kong. Lana's great grandfather, Cheung Kai, was a developer who owned a lot of properties where the old Kai Tak Airport was located. Her ancestors first started in Shandong and moved down to Chong San in Guangdong province centuries ago, making them Cantonese with Chong San as their *laojia*, or home village.

Lana's father was one of six boys, including his two nephews who were older than him, to study in England in the 1890s. He went on to Cambridge to study and he also took up flying, a rare feat at that time. When the First World War broke out he was recalled to Hong Kong, as his widowed mother did not want her only son to participate in the war. He saw love at first sight when he met Lucy Sim playing tennis at St. Stephen School, and he subsequently married her on March 28, 1918. They had six children: Peter, Madeline, Gladys, Johnny, Rita and, lastly, Lana. He became a real estate developer building his own family residences, such as their home at 7 College Road and their weekend place at Ting Kau, as well as developing their properties on Glenealy and Cockrane Streets. He went every weekday to the Chinese Club to have lunch and trade gossip with his friends. He was affectionately known as "Uncle," even by people older than himself.

He was distinguished looking, standing very erect with his grey hair carefully trimmed. He was always immaculately dressed with a tie or a cravat and a hat. He enjoyed his English habits, such as having tea, carrying an umbrella or wearing a cravat. Besides being active in the Chinese Club, he was also active as a board member of the Hong Kong Housing Society, a semi-government body that provides low-cost housing. For his contribution to the Housing Society, the Society named one of their estates in Hunghom, Gar Hing Estate, after him. He was the first Chinese committee member at St. Johns Cathedral, a founding member of Christ Church in Kowloon Tong, a trustee of the Christ Church School, and a founding member of the Kowloon Tong Club.

Lana's mother was a person who did not hide her emotions. When I first came to Hong Kong, she would hardly speak to me and I thought she couldn't speak English. Then I thought she was against me because I was of Japanese race and her memories of the war were so unpleasant. A week after I arrived, I came down with a bad case of the flu, probably caused by a combination of travel fatigue and active socializing, then further triggered by some hot and spicy Malaysian food I was not used to. I was in bed with fever in the hotel with no one to take care of me, as Lana had to work. So her mother, who was afraid that I might die in Hong Kong, started looking after me, bringing me lunch every day and giving me medicine. After that, she and I became the best of friends and I later became her favourite son-in-law.

She was born as Lucy Hung Hing Sim, in Singapore, but grew up in Swatow with her foster father, who was the local compradore for Jardine, a large British trading company. There she lived like a princess, spoiled by her father, and traveling all over the world with him. Her stepbrother, the late George Sim, was active in trading Swatow lace in Hong Kong. His wife Charlotte is still alive and now lives in Toronto. Their four sons all live in North America. One of the sons, Alfred, is close to Lana and keeps in touch with her. Lucy Sim came to study at St. Stephens School in Hong Kong, where she met Andrew. In her teens she was very pretty and popular and many of her friends wanted her to be their brides-maid.

On July 14, 1960, I stayed behind after lunch to talk to Lana's parents about her hand in marriage. I had waited four months for this moment and I was nervous. I asked Lana's mother if I could speak to them both, but she excused herself and then came back to say that she would speak for both of them. I asked her for Lana's hand and she was very frank in her reply. Her main concern was whether or not Lana and I could get along together. I guess word of my proposal had spread fast, as that afternoon at tea, Madeline and Gladys were calling me "brother-in-law." On August 25, 1960, Lana's grandmother passed away. She was 92. Lana and her sister Rita were both very close to her and her death affected them a great deal. After observing an appropriate mourning period following the funeral, we decided to get married in the spring of the next year.

During this period, I was doing some consulting work for the Chung brothers, owners of what is now known as the Hyatt Regency Hotel. The architect was the late Jackson Wong, whom I had met when I came to Hong Kong, and whom I considered at that time to be the best architect in Hong Kong. However, because of my previous experience in designing Sheraton hotels, the Chung brothers asked me to be their consultant, an offer that I accepted. I immediately went to see Jackson to explain the situation and he accepted my role. This is where my experience with Sheraton paid off. I found the hotel to be generally workable except for the matter of its function in a few of the service areas. The income from this consultancy certainly helped toward our honeymoon expenses.

At our wedding reception, from left to right: Frank Kwok, Git Ming Fu, Nesbert Kwong, Janet Eng (Maid of Honour), Lana's father, Lana, JHK, Lana's mother, Samuel Wong and Joseph Li (Best Man).

10

Marriage

We got married on March 18, 1961, at Christ Church in Kowloon Tong. Canon Martin officiated at the ceremony. Joseph Li was my best man with Nesbert Kwong, Samual Wong and Frank Kwok as my ushers. Lana had Janet Eng as her Maid of Honour and her niece, Git Ming, as her bridesmaid. Lana looked gorgeous in her wedding gown, which had been designed by a friend, a well-known designer from the USA, Gladis Moy.

It was a beautiful day and the atmosphere in Christ Church, with Lana's friends and relatives, was perfect for the occasion. The church was filled with orchids, sent from Singapore by Richard Eu from the garden of Monica Chan, sister of Lee Kuan Yiu. After the wedding, we held a reception for the guests from the church wedding. It was held at the home of Gladys and Lai Yuen Leung at No. 1 College Road, located just around the corner from the church. I am now gazing at the photograph taken in the garden of the Leung residence with Lana's parents, best man and the ushers as well as the bridesmaids. Everybody looks so young, especially Lana's parents. That evening there was a Chinese banquet for

500 people in the ballroom of the Miramar Hotel. We designed the cake like a church with the gothic arches spanning across it, a gift from Young Chi Wan, the Miramar's owner.

Our honeymoon trip to Europe was not only a honeymoon but also a tour of architecture that we were supposed to see over a year ago. I took two months off from work, thanks to the understanding partners of Palmer and Turner. We first flew to Istanbul on Pan American Flight 1, which took 18 hours. During those days, the flights were not very full so we were able to sleep by taking three seats together to lie down, before our arrival at 9:00 a.m. We stayed at the Istanbul Hilton, which was the best hotel at that time.

Next day, we took a taxi to see the Blue Mosque and Santa Sophia. As we were getting close to Santa Sophia, I noticed a familiar face in the taxi next to us. When we alighted, we were joined by Professor Bush Brown who taught history of architecture at MIT. What good luck to have him with us to describe the architecture of Santa Sophia! However, we were more impressed with the space and atmosphere of the Blue Mosque, even though architecturally speaking, Santa Sophia is more significant. As we removed our shoes and entered the Blue Mosque, we were mesmerized by the mysterious blue atmosphere of the enormous space under the dome. We wandered around in a daze, as though we were in a dream. The walls were covered in blue paint and tiles with stained glass windows punctuating the walls to let in the small amount of light that penetrated into the dark space. Chandeliers, which hovered close to the ground, hung down from the high ceiling to create a sparkle of tiny lights, like those seen from a plane while landing in a city at night.

The Blue Mosque's real name is Sultan Ahmet Mosque, and it was built in the years 1608 to 1614 by the architect Sedefkar Mehmet Aga. It is not a particularly noteworthy architectural example in terms of size, age or merit, but the space made a deep impression upon us. The plan is very simple, an exact square with a central dome, 77 feet in diameter, on massive circular columns, surrounded by semicircular domes making the total space 155 feet across.

In Vienna we indulged in some opera, seeing the *Barber of Seville* and the *Bartered Bride* at the Staatsoper. Afterwards we treated ourselves to a romantic dinner with candlelight and piano music, for a fitting memory of Vienna. The next day, we bought a lamb fur coat for Lana and, in the evening, we joined a tour, "Vienna at Night," where they took us to the outskirts of the city to view the city at night, but it was nothing compared to the night scene of Hong Kong. We went to the wine village of Grinzig for sausage and wine and finally ended up in "Moulin Rouge," where we saw striptease after striptease but it became so monotonous that I fell asleep. I also bought Lana a large heart-shaped pastry with the German words "eternally yours," which we kept for many years.

At Salzburg, we stayed at Hotel Stein and had dinner at Goldener Hirsch. After that it was off to Innsbruck, but we found that the people were not very friendly and the ski slopes were out of town, so we took a train to St. Anton in the Arlberg to ski. We got up early the next morning to rent our skis and boots and went to classes. Lana took the beginner class and I took the intermediate. Lana became very tired of lugging her skis around in her heavy boots. The snow was fast melting and it rained in the lower slopes so we had to go higher up. It wasn't much of a honeymoon, skiing separately during the day and so tired in the evening that we went to sleep right after dinner. We stayed in St. Anton for nine days, but as the snow was disappearing fast, it was time to leave.

In the last few days there were no ski classes, so we toured the surrounding ski areas and visited Lech and Zurs, where we were to return later in our lives. We were sorry to leave St. Anton. We boarded a train where we met a helpful German couple who were on their way to Hamburg; they insisted that we must see Munich and got us a hotel when the train stopped in Munich. We found

Munich to be a delightful city to walk around in. By this time we were craving Chinese food and finally found a restaurant. We promised ourselves that we would return to Munich, which we have done many times since.

In Copenhagen we went to Oskar Davidson for a smorgasbord dinner, ordering from a four-foot long menu. Lana also made some purchases of fabric for Peck and Wilson. We then went to London, which was my first time there. We did the usual tourist route, visiting the Tate Gallery and attending services at St. Paul's Cathedral; we had a wonderful experience listening to the Berlin Philharmonic with Von Karajan conducting at the Royal Festival Hall. I liked London very much; little did we realize then that it would later become our second home.

The morning of our departure, we decided to have breakfast in bed, just like the honeymooners you see in the movies. The breakfast arrived on a tray so we put it on the bed and tried to crawl back into the bed so the tray would end up on our laps. It wasn't as easy as we thought and a slight movement made the coffee spill all over the white sheets. That promptly ended our romantic notions of breakfast in bed. We wrote a note to apologize for the mess and quickly checked out to take a flight to Paris.

We stayed in a small pleasant hotel in Montmartre for 14 francs per night. However, there was only a basin and the toilet in the room, with the bath located in the hallway outside of our room. To use the bath, you had to pay for and book it. So we would book for only one person and the other would quickly sneak in when the first had finished using the bath, thus saving the cost of a second person. Although Montmartre is touristy, it has a local community of its own with a market and restaurants, one with which we became so familiar that the proprietress would hug us every time we went there to dine. We thoroughly enjoyed our stay there.

We picked up a car, a Peugeot 404, and drove to Chartres, Versailles and

Fontainebleau before heading to Lyon and to Avignon, stopping to see Corbusier's convent at Eveux l'Arbresle. I was impressed by his bold use of forms and the honest use of concrete. At Marseilles, we saw Corbusier's Unite l'Habitation and I was surprised by its misleading scale. I asked Lana to pose by the external staircase and waited for her to appear above the railing. After waiting for some time, I shouted for her to hurry up; then her hand appeared above the railing, waving to signal where she was. The railing was higher than the height of a person and was there just to give a solid feel to the external staircase. I then realized that Corbusier's work was about form and not about human scale.

We found St. Tropez delightful and decided to stay a few days. We went

Lana skiing at St. Anton

for a swim, but the water was freezing, not like the waters of Hong Kong. Lana looked good in a bikini, but here in St. Tropez nobody takes notice as they are so commonly worn. We then went on to Cannes and Nice, stopping to have lunch in Eze, a picturesque town perched on top of a cliff. We saw Matisse Chapel in Vence and bought perfumes at Gourdon. After trying our luck at the gambling tables of Monte Carlo (we weren't lucky), we drove to Italy to see the famed flower garden of St. Remo and bought four dozen red roses for Lana—they were so cheap.

Genoa was dirty, noisy and confusing; it took four hours to make arrangements to ship our car to Hong Kong at the end of the trip. After visiting picturesque Portofino and St. Margarita, we had to go to Pisa to see the leaning tower. It was hectic driving into Florence, which was noisy and disorganized. After driving around in circles, we finally found a nice hotel overlooking Ponte Vecchio. We walked up the 414 steps to the Campanile designed by Giotto and looked down to see Queen Elizabeth drive by. We walked all over the city, finding it to be a city suitable in scale for walking, and we visited the usual sights— Medici Chapel, Uffizi Gallery, Santa Croce, and the Four Davids. We liked the one by Donatello the best. Then we drove on to Rome, stopping at Siena and San Gimignano.

In Rome we called up John Morphett, a former classmate from MIT, who was now working for Gropius of the Architect Collaborative at the University of Baghdad in Rome. John had recently retired from Hassel and Partners in Adelaide, where he was the principal, and was awarded the prestigious Gold Medal from the Royal Australian Institute of Architects. He took us in his Volkswagen van, along with his wife Vivienne and two sons Jonathan and Adrian, all over Rome, where we saw Boromino's church, St. Paul-outside-the-walls Basilica, Nervi's Palazzo de Sport, EUR and so many other places that I cannot remember. We had a very nice lunch at Castelgandolfo, the summer residence of the Pope, located just outside of Rome.

One evening, John and Vivienne took us to Da Meo Patacca, a gay and boisterous restaurant located in an old grotto that was full of atmosphere and fun. We shall always treasure the hospitality he and his family extended to us during our stay in Rome. Harry Kiyooka, my artist friend from Manitoba days, was living in a picturesque hill town named Anticoli Corrado, just outside Rome, a little further than Tivoli. We went to visit him, talked about old times and viewed his paintings. It was so good to see him again.

Our next destination was Venice, with a stop at Assisi along the way. We were impressed with the way San Francisco of Assisi was sited in a dramatic position and, together with its famous Giotto murals, we found it one of the most interesting buildings on our trip. In Arezzo, we got up early to view the frescoes of Piero della Francesca in the strong morning light, but even then they appeared quite dark. However, seeing these frescoes made us more appreciative of his work.

At Ravenna, we saw the Byzantine mosaics, which looked as fresh as the day they were laid. Venice is supposed to be the honeymooners' dream, but for me it was a nightmare. I ate too much Italian food and got sick. We had dinner in our hotel, which had a fixed menu. After the appetizers came the pasta, my favourite food. I finished it ravenously along with Lana's portion, since she wasn't very hungry. I thought the pasta was the main course, as was the custom at home in Canada. But to my surprise, the veal came out as the main course; not wanting to waste anything, I finished it as well as the cheese and desert that followed. I was so full that I felt uncomfortable, and of course the wine did not help. That night, I developed a high fever and felt so sick that I thought I was going to die. (At least dying would relieve me of this terrible pain.) I told Lana what she should do if I died and gave her the plane ticket and all the money.

Lana was terrified of the situation and wondered what to do. It was too late to call a doctor. In the middle of the night all my food came back up, enough to fill the whole basin in the bathroom. The next day, I still felt weak with fever so I stayed in bed all day. The following day, I tried to venture out, but it was raining hard, and when it rains in Venice, everything disappears— people, gondoliers, sidewalk cafes, outdoor concerts, lights—making it a deserted and depressing city. This was our sorry memory of Venice.

From Venice we drove to Padua to see Giotto's frescoes and then on to Verona for a bit of Romeo and Juliet. It was pouring when we got to Milan, where we booked our air and train tickets to go home. We also visited Pino, where we met one of the young men that took care of Lana when she was in Cortina over four years ago; he was now at the Air Academy doing his military service.

We had a wonderful time on our honeymoon, enjoying the simple pleasures of life as well as the opportunities to see many of the European buildings I had wanted to visit since I first studied architecture. Unfortunately, the trip was marred by the loss of all photographic records of our trip. In Rome, I took the rolls of films to a photo shop for developing. When they came back, they were all a bluish tint. They had developed the photos as black and white instead of colour.

11

Palmer and Turner

About four months after I arrived in Hong Kong, I went to a party where Andrew Eu happened to mention that the firm of Palmer and Turner had obtained the job of designing a hotel on a recently auctioned site on Murray Parade Grounds. With my experience in hotel design, I thought this could be a job opportunity for me, so I went, without an appointment, to the offices of Palmer and Turner, then located in the old Hong Kong and Shanghai Bank Building. Palmer and Turner had started up in 1868 and when I first approached its offices, it was well established as one of the oldest British architectural and engineering firms. Palmer and Turner has designed many of the major buildings in Hong Kong as well as those buildings that still remain on the Bund in Shanghai, such as the Hong Kong and Shanghai Bank Building, Bank of China, Bank of Mitsui, Peace Hotel, Palace Hotel, Cathay Mansions, Broadway Mansions, the Jewish Synagogue and many other prominent buildings.

I took the lift up to the third floor and entered a dark and gloomy corridor to search for the small brass nameplate of Palmer and Turner. I opened the door and entered into a drab reception room. Behind the high counter sat a rather small Chinese lady (Miss Yip) with glasses perched on her tiny nose and who was busy typing a letter.

"Excuse me," I said.

"Yes, what can I do for you," she replied as she peered over the counter.

"I would like to see Mr. Palmer." I had pulled up all my courage. In my student days I was told to always see the top man for job interviews.

"Oh, Mr. Palmer has been gone for a long time," the lady giggled.

"Can I see Mr. Turner then?" I then asked, undaunted.

"Oh, he has also been gone for a long time." She giggled even more.

"Then can I see whoever is the head of the firm?"

"Mr. Smart is the senior partner, but he is out of town at the moment. Would you like to see Mr. Campbell, who is a junior partner?"

I thought that if this was the best they could do, I might as well see him. "Fine," I said.

Soon there appeared a lanky gaunt-looking Scotsman with blonde hair and a slight limp, who interviewed me. I think he was relieved to meet someone with knowledge of designing hotels, as the firm had no recent experience in planning hotels. I was fortunate to be interviewed by Ian Campbell, as he is truly a gentleman and a fine person. He took me in and it was to be a lifetime commitment.

Ian J. Campbell was born in England but his family originated in Scotland. He served in the Navy during the war and received a wound in his leg, which gave him trouble for a long time, even after I met him. He studied architecture after the war, as a veteran, and came to Hong Kong to join Palmer and Turner, becoming a partner in 1959. He loved sailing and kept a boat at the Royal Hong Kong Yacht Club, going on a cruise every weekend. He did not race—he was not that sort of person.

Everybody liked him, especially the staff, and clients trusted him for his honesty and integrity. He and I worked very well as a team and we never had any disagreements. However, there was one occasion when we were talking about future partners. He felt that the most important factor for choosing a partner was character. I thought it was the ability to design. Looking back, I now feel that Ian was right. Design ability is important but the most important factor is the character of the person.

I started work at Palmer and Turner on Monday, July 18, 1961. The office was very busy with the new hotel project. Ian Campbell was the partner in charge and I was assigned as the project designer and architect. The clients were two Texans, Corrigan and Wynn, who had won the auction for the site with a record bid. Their requirement was to have a 1000-room hotel with two floors for a shopping arcade. In order to accommodate a large number of rooms on such a tight site, I came up with a "T-shaped" plan that met their requirements, and they liked it. I placed the hotel above the two floors of the shopping arcade, with the lobby on the third level, which forced all the guests to go through the shopping area.

I placed the swimming pool on the roof of the podium and arranged two floors of rooms around the pool calling it cabanas like a beach resort in order to fit in 1000 rooms. It was frustrating to fight for space especially around the entry driveway on the ground floor. I felt it was important to project a feeling of welcome for those arriving at the hotel and to make sure that cars and tour buses did not cause congestion in the area. I lost the battle, however, as the Texans wanted more shop space on the prime ground floor area.

Once the preliminary drawings were approved, we worked very hard to complete the contract drawings by September. Corrigan and Wynn were due back in Hong Kong in early September to sign the contract with Paul Y Construction Co. It was an unusual way of settling a contract. There was no tender.

Paul Y was selected as the contractor even before they bid for the site. In fact, it was Paul Y who introduced the site to the Texans and gave them information to prepare for bidding on the site. When they won the bid, they asked Paul Y to recommend architects, and Paul Y recommended Palmer and Turner.

With time as the most important factor, we had to prepare the contract documents in one and a half months. All we could do was to prepare a few sheets of A3-sized, 1/32-scaled plans, along with elevations and sections with some detail drawings, such as the typical bedrooms and a set of outline specifications. Based on that, Paul Y had to come up with a contract price. There were no building quantities and no steel quantities, just a table of finishes and outline specifications.

On September 8, the contract was signed between Wynncor and Paul Y for 25 million Hong Kong dollars. Next came the difficult task of preparing detailed drawings that would stay within the contract price. Of course, as time went on and details were produced, Paul Y protested loudly that he was losing money, since he had underestimated the quantity of steel; he asked for additional sums to which we sympathetically gave support. However, our support was not made any easier when Paul Y, in his usual flamboyant fashion, had to show off his new acquisition—a Rolls Royce—used when he went to the airport to pick up the Texans on their periodic visits.

I worked full time on the hotel project, then known as the American Hotel, later changed to the Hong Kong Hilton after the Texans negotiated a management contract with Hilton. Its competition was the Mandarin Hotel, which was being developed by Hong Kong Land and designed by Leigh and Orange. Howard Baron was our project manager, so it was with him that I worked most closely during this period, unless the Corrigans and the Wynns were in town.

Opposite page: Hilton Hotel. (Photo courtesy of P&T Group.)

Howard was a small man who was involved in the oil business in Texas where he got to know the Corrigans. He was very fair with me and supported whatever I proposed. After he finished the Hilton Hotel, he went into business on his own in Hong Kong, which was rather mysterious. He was murdered with a bullet in his head one New Year's eve as he sat in his office in Hong Kong; the case has never been solved.

Dale and Pat Keller, a husband-and-wife team who were practicing in Japan, were selected as the interior designers. Their designs set high standards for hotel interiors in Asia and many of their former employees, after training in their company, became leading designers in Asia. Henry Steiner was the graphic designer and was responsible for the huge HH logo on the podium of the hotel. Initially it was AH but later, when Hilton accepted the management contract, it was an easy task to change from AH to HH. Lana also got involved by designing some of the shops in the arcade for Air India and other clients. It was a good team and we all worked very well together. When it was nearing completion, it was funny to see two very pregnant women walking on the site, supervising the work. At the time, Lana was carrying her unborn son and Pat Keller was also expecting a boy. (Coincidentally, both babies would be named Andrew.)

Just before Christmas, after the contract was signed, Paul Y asked for me to see him at his office. I thought nothing of it, as we had met many times before to discuss the project. He asked me what I wanted for Christmas or, rather, how I wanted it? I was taken aback and stammered that I did not want anything nor did I expect anything. I reported this encounter to Ian Campbell immediately and I think he appreciated it. Later, when I became the senior partner, I made a ruling that at Christmas, when contractors and suppliers tended to send their greetings in goods, that we would not accept any gifts or payments, other than perishables such as fruits, as a sign of goodwill. It was the way Hong Kong worked.

The hotel was finally finished in 1962, and Conrad Hilton himself came for the opening. It was a tradition for the Chinese to let off firecrackers for good luck. So a long string of firecrackers was suspended from the top of the building and lit at the bottom; as the firecrackers were lit, the string of firecrackers was lowered so that the firing always took place near the ground where it would be safe. However the main air intake for the air conditioning system for the public areas was next to the place where the firecrackers were being lit, so the smoke from the bursting firecrackers was sucked into the hotel. The lobby and the ballroom where the ceremony was to take place became full of acrid smoke from the firecrackers and we could hardly see each other, let alone stand the smell. We all had to wait outside until all of the firecrackers had been fired off and fresh air recirculated through the system before the ceremony could begin.

The Hong Kong Hilton is no longer there. In 1996, the new owners of the site, Cheung Kong, tore it down and built an office building on the site. A familiar story in Hong Kong.

When I was busy with the Hilton, the office was busy with the design of Choi Hung Estate and Prince's Building. During the postwar period from 1946 to 1960, the population of Hong Kong doubled with the huge influx of refugees from China after the takeover by the communists. Many squatters were living in wooden or tin shacks on the hillside, at the mercy of landslides caused by heavy rainfall, or torn apart by the raging typhoons so prevalent during the summer. Many of these squatters had no sewage, no electricity, no water, and no road access. This tremendous influx of refugees created an acute shortage of hous- ing, which prompted the government to build basic housing to accommodate these people. Initially, to meet this crisis, resettlement estates were hastily built to provide rooms for individual families. These were six-storey walk-ups with com- munal toilets.

Choi Hung Estate was a low-cost housing project built through the

Housing Authority for 22,000 people. It was designed by the team of Ian Campbell and Dick Pang. Later, each unit was designed to include an attached toilet and kitchen, setting a new standard for low-cost housing in Hong Kong. Following completion, it was awarded the prestigious HKIA Silver Medal in 1965.

Prince's Building is one of the buildings owned by Hong Kong Land, a major developer in the central business district and our major client. This building was designed by Ian Campbell and Jimmy Ouyang and was completed in 1963. It was unique, in that the external cladding was made up of pre-cast concrete sections with the polished terrazzo finish integrated into the sections, which enabled rapid completion of the building. The General Manager of Hong Kong Land at that time was Bevin Fields who believed in having strong corners on his buildings—hence the solid windowless corners on Prince's Building and also on the Mandarin Hotel. As it was designed based on the old volume calculation, which exceeds the present calculation by a plot ratio that is based on floor area, it probably will not ever be redeveloped. This is true for many of the buildings in Hong Kong.

In 1963, after the Hilton Hotel was completed, the firm offered me a partnership. I wasn't sure whether I wanted to stay in Hong Kong for the rest of my life, as I felt that Hong Kong did not have the right environment to encourage good design. The clients in general were not interested in promoting the best design solutions, but were more interested in squeezing in every square foot of space that was permitted under the regulations, while completing projects as cheaply and as quickly as possible. The government also contributed to this lack of good design by enforcing rigid regulations designed to prevent illegal or inappropriate use of any additional space that developers might try to squeeze out. This made it very restrictive for freedom of expression. Therefore, I talked to Lana and we agreed that we should visit Canada and the United States to see if we wanted to start a new life there or to return to Hong Kong and accept the partnership.

In mid September 1963, Lana and I set off on a round-the-world trip lasting almost three months. The intentions were to take a well-earned holiday, to investigate possibilities for our future living arrangements, and to see our old friends again. We left our firstborn son, Andrew, under the care of Lana's mother and flew off to Sydney, and then to Fiji, where we stayed in a thatch-roofed cottage by the reef. We took our first snorkelling lessons from a Fijian called Walleye, whose feet were so big he didn't need any flippers to go diving. He was also big in body, which may have explained why he could hold his breath for so long under-water. He taught us many things about the sea—how to open and eat sea urchins and how to avoid lionfish.

Fiji was an idyllic place, very popular with the Australians, but we found that it rained too much. We later moved from Papeete, the capital of Tahiti, to the neighbouring island of Moorea, on which it is said that the movie *South Pacific* was based. The hotel there also had grass-roofed cottages along the beach. The problem with these grass roofs is that they harbour a lot of insects in the grass, which attract lizards and geckos. One night after we turned the lights off, something dropped on my face and kept moving. We turned on the lights and found a gecko eating a huge spider above our bed and every time he took a bite, one of the legs of the spider would drop off onto my face with the leg still wriggling. Since we could not get the gecko to move, we had to move the bed.

Moorea is a small island with beautiful beaches all around the island and dramatic mountain ranges in the middle of the island. After a few days of swimming, snorkelling and lying on the beach, we got so bored that I challenged Lana to ride a bicycle around the island and, if she succeeded, I would buy her a fur coat. After an early lunch, we started off, first along a well-used dirt road, which soon disappeared into the sand along the beach and into the crossing along the many streams. The path that looked easy at first became more difficult and involved pushing the bicycle through the soft sand along the beach and fording the streams. It soon became dark and we were only two thirds of the way home. Soon we came to a store in the middle of nowhere and found out the owners were Chinese. Lana was relieved. We soon made friends with them and got them to take us back to the hotel in their pickup, for a price of course. For the Chinese, no matter where they are, money talks. Although technically we did not finish going around the island on the bicycle, I still bought Lana a fur coat, later in our trip, for her effort.

We went to Slocan to visit my parents and my grandfather. My father met us at Castlegar airport and drove us to Slocan. When we passed through Popoff, or stopped to see a view of Little Slocan Valley, memories of my youth would flood through my mind. I realized that I missed nature and the outdoor life. So during our short stay, I tried to relive my youth by going hunting for *matsutake*, the precious Japanese mushroom, with Grandpa, who had moved back to Canada when Grandmother passed away in 1961. He led the way, and when he saw the telltale sign of a mound on the pine leaves, he would point his stick and call Lana. Lana would then carefully dig around the mound to reveal a family of *matsutakes*. As the only word Lana ever heard my Grandfather say was her name, Lana thought he could not speak any English, until on the final day, he said to her in perfect English, "Lana, I hope you will come back to Slocan to see me again soon." He was a man of few words but he got along great with Lana.

In Winnipeg, Lana wanted to go back and see our old university, and especially to return a favourite café near the university, called Van Buren, which served delicious pork chops. She used to go there regularly with her friends whenever they got tired of the food in the residence. To her great disappointment, however, it didn't live up to her expectations. Had she thought so highly about it in her memory, because it was such a treat compared to the bland residence food, or had her standards gone up since then?

The Red River that once looked so romantic when we strolled hand in hand was only a brown river flowing around the campus—the magic was gone. Sometimes I think it is better just to remember the past and not try to recreate those precious memories by revisiting it.

While in Toronto I went to see some architects for job prospects. We stayed with Gene, my brother, who was now married with a baby son. We should have gone to a hotel, because staying with family was a mistake. After Lana helped with the cooking, did the dishes and cleaned up the house, she decided that life in Canada was not for her.

We next travelled to Cairo, where we met Pete DiTullio who set up the management of the Hong Kong Hilton and was now head of the Middle East operations for Hilton. We were staying in a modest hotel but he insisted upon our staying at the Hilton; he arranged a car to pick us up and installed us in the presidential suite of the hotel. It had separate bedrooms for the man and the woman, and there was a guard standing at the doorway 24 hours a day. Our resources at that time were limited, and we were afraid to spend money on food and souvenirs as the cost of the presidential suite itself would more than eat up our budget. What a relief it was when we checked out and found that we did not have to pay a cent for our stay at the Hilton. We wrote a letter of thanks to Pete and we shall always be grateful to him for his generosity. He later became the head of Hyatt Hotels and passed away shortly afterwards.

We made our way up the Nile to Upper Egypt to see the impressive temple of Karnak with its huge columns. After visiting the Valley of the Kings, we wanted to see the temple of Queen Hatshepsut, and were told that the quickest way there was to take a mule over the hill to the next valley. It may be the quickest way, but certainly it wasn't the easiest way as we sat on the mule, in the heat, climbing up the rocky path. However, the view from the top was worth the effort before we scampered down to the Temple of Queen Hatshepsut. That evening, when we got back to the hotel, a group of American tourists were talking in hushed voices so we asked them what had happened. They told us that President Kennedy had just been assassinated.

India had always fascinated me, so I was looking forward to seeing it. At Bombay, we met Jal Cowasji, the Art Director for Air India; Lana had gotten to know him when she was working at the ticket office for Air India in the Hong Kong Hilton. Jal was a stout Parsee with a swooping moustache, which made him look very much like the bowing Maharajah, the symbol of Air India. He took us to the antique markets of Bombay where we saw a beautiful 10th-century Pala sculpture of Avalokiteshvara. Jal said it was a museum piece and recommended that we buy it.

We started bargaining hard to get the price that we thought we could afford with our limited capital. After the price was settled, the dealer then said we could not take the piece out of the country as it is considered a national treasure. As we had set our hearts upon it, that was a blow to us. Then Jal spoke to the man to see if there was any way of getting it out of the country, and he said he would investigate. The next day, the dealer explained that he would ship the piece in a trunk to a shop in Hong Kong, as part of their consignment, but we would have to pay for the arrangements. It finally ended up that the cost of shipping, packing and getting it out of the country cost more than the sculpture. We were trapped, as we couldn't very well bargain on a cost when we had no idea of what it should be. We accepted because we loved the piece so much, and it was delivered safely to Hong Kong where we made payment upon delivery. It is still displayed proudly in our home.

After visiting the fabulous caves of Ajanta and Ellora, we made preparations to go to New Delhi. Jal told us that we must go to Agra to see the Taj Mahal, especially as we would be there during the full moon. We were not planning to see the Taj, as we thought it was just a tourist trap, but after Jal's urging, we decided to go. We are so glad that we did. We were amazed at how beautiful the building is. It is symmetrical, with its exotic shape in white marble, reflected in the formal pool, with fountains in the huge entrance court. It was perfect in its proportions and, from a distance, looked unreal, like an architectural model. We returned that evening to view it under the full moon. It was surreal; the building was bathed in a cool blue moonlight that exposed every mortar joint in the marble. It looked completely different in the moonlight than in sunlight. With its perfection of symmetry, beauty of design and delicate decoration, it is no wonder that it is so admired.

The Taj Mahal is a mausoleum built in the years 1630 to 1653 by Shah Jahan in memory of his favourite wife, Mumtaz-i-Mahal. The building is 186 feet square, with splayed angles crowned with a dominant bulbous dome rising nearly 200 feet above the platform. It sits on an 18-foot high platform, which is 315 feet square with 133-foot high minarets on each corner. The surface of the white marble is inlaid with semiprecious stones in shapes of scrolls, fretwork and wreaths.

We were away for almost three months. We enjoyed India much more than Egypt, mainly because of the attitude of the people. In Egypt, everybody was demanding *baksheesh*, which made it annoying and unpleasant. It was hot, dirty and full of flies everywhere we went, which added to the annoyance. In India, you would also find beggars and poor children, but they did not demand money; instead they smiled at you to win your affection. People were much friendlier in India and this made us feel welcome rather than ripped off, as in Egypt. We have returned to India many times but we have not gone back to Egypt, nor do we particularly want to.

Once we were back in Hong Kong, we had to decide whether or not to accept the offer of the partnership with Palmer and Turner. One of the offers in America was to head the architectural division of Hilton, an offer made by Pete Ditul-

lio. However, Lana was not keen on the North American way of life. As for my concerns that Hong Kong did not care for good design and was a cultural desert, Lana argued that it would be a challenge and that I should accept it and do something about it, rather than trying to escape from it. I must say that she had a point and, with her resistance to returning to North America, I decided to stay in Hong Kong, taking the challenge Lana described and accepting the partnership with Palmer and Turner.

It was then that C. V. Starr, of American International Assurance, called me in to design a new headquarters for AIA. C. V. Starr started his insurance business in Shanghai and built it up to be one of the biggest insurance companies in the world. He supported many charities, especially those that helped young Asians get further education in America. He was interested in architecture and I think that subconsciously he wanted to be an architect, himself, so he turned to me as a means of fulfilling his dream.

I designed a simple rectangular tower with the external columns to take the load of the building; glass windows were located behind the external columns. No other client in Hong Kong would ever allow this as they considered it to be a waste of space, but the Building Authority assisted by calculating the ratio of gross floor area to the glass line instead of to the structural columns outside the line of the windows. I also think that the government was lenient in their interpretation, as they imposed a plot ratio of three instead of the usual ten, saying that it would affect the traffic flow on that corner.

There was a bit of controversy when people remarked that the space between the structural columns resembled a coffin and created bad *feng shui*. Structurally, a post tensioning system was used on the beams to make the long span more effective. The external columns were designed as pre-cast units to permit a

Opposite page: AIA Building. (Photo courtesy of P&T Group.)

faster construction time, but Paul Y Construction Company opted for the traditional poured-in-place system, to which we could not object as they said it would be cheaper. This building won the HKIA Silver medal Award in 1969.

In the sixties, I had the luxury of not only designing but also carrying out an entire project on my own from beginning to end. Ian Campbell was the partner in charge and he handled the client relationship and the meetings with the Building Authority, leaving me to concentrate on the design development, detailing and supervision of the project. However, after Ian Campbell moved to Australia in 1968 to head the office there, I had to do the job that he used to do, which left very little time for me to carry out projects from beginning to end. Therefore, we would set up teams led by either Malcolm Purvis or me, as we were the two architectural partners. The team would be comprised of a project architect who would look after all the administrative aspects of the project and would be responsible for it from beginning to completion. Initial design would be done mainly by the partner in charge, ably assisted by the project architect, but sometimes, we would call for design ideas from everyone in the office and review those ideas. During the initial concept, we would also get together with the structural engineers to discuss integration of the structural concepts for the project.

The design process this became a matter of teamwork, with many people getting involved, and this strengthened the final solution. Although one person may have had a brilliant solution, it was only through teamwork that it would become a reality. I think this is where the strength of Palmer and Turner lies.

12

The riots of 1967

In 1966, China started the Cultural Revolution, causing terrible upheaval to the whole nation. Children turned against their parents, students turned against their teachers and the workers turned against the intellectuals. It caused total chaos in China—burning of books, destruction of antiques, beating of people, ransacking of homes, school and university closures, and persecution of anyone who had a capitalist history.

In 1967 the Cultural Revolution soon spilled into Hong Kong, which was hit with riots and bombings that led to curfews and emergency measures. Many were maimed by bomb blasts and 51 people died. It was the worst unrest Hong Kong had ever experienced. This adversely affected our work and we were concerned with the future of Hong Kong. New work stopped coming in, but fortunately we had enough existing jobs to keep going. At that time, the Hong Kong Electric Headquarters and Transmission Station and Century Tower were just being designed and both projects were going ahead in spite of the riots. In fact, these projects benefited from the low construction costs caused by the distur-

1967 – First visit to Hong Kong. Back, left to right: Mother, Grandfather Maikawa, JHK, Lana, Father. Front: Andrew and Yuri.

bance.

Nonetheless, we felt that we had all our eggs in one basket and were too dependent on the fortunes of Hong Kong. To remedy the situation, we started to look beyond our boundaries to other countries.

Fortunately, Hong Kong Land also had similar thoughts of expanding abroad and asked us to design the Australian Club Building in Sydney, Australia. We jumped at the chance and decided to set up an office in Sydney where I spent two summers with my family; I also took many more trips to Sydney during the design and development period of this project. Ian Campbell, who also spent a lot of time in Sydney, finally decided to move there permanently to head the office. The local architects selected were from the firm of Lionel Todd, which was one of the firms that carried out the work on the Sydney Opera House after the original architect, Jorn Utzon, left. The structural engineer was Paul Hagenbach, of Connell and Hagenbach.

The arrangement that H K Land made with the Australian Club was similar to the arrangement made later with the H K Club in Hong Kong. H K Land would provide temporary premises for the Australian Club until the building was finished, then move them to their new premises, all at H K Land's expense. In return, the Australian Club would permit H K Land to redevelop the site, build an office building above the club, rent the office space and share the rental income from the office space for a certain period of time. After the expiry of that term, the office space would revert back to the club and they would enjoy the full rental income from the office space. The Australian Club could not lose by such a deal.

I designed the building as layers of three slabs, with the two outer slabs forming useable space and the middle slab accommodating the core with lifts, staircases, toilets, air conditioning rooms, etc. Each slab sets back from the other to fit into the corner, which is at an angle, with the entrance to the club located on the central slab, to create a welcoming feeling. The club was accommodated on the lower floors with the office space above. After discussing the design with the structural engineers, we decided to use pre-cast panels for the exterior, using their local sandstone as the aggregate for the finish. After the Australian Club was finished, the office was quite busy with all sorts of proposals, as the Australians love to speculate. None of these schemes materialized, however, and we soon had to close the office, and Ian Campbell moved back to Hong Kong.

I first saw the Sydney Opera House when it was still under construction in 1968, the same year that we went to set up our office in Sydney to design the Australian Club. In 1966 Utzon withdrew from the project under unhappy circumstances because his fees were not paid due to a great many misunderstandings regarding time and budget. The responsibility to complete the project was transferred to a group of Australian firms who tried to carry out the design intent of Utzon. Only very recently, after 35 years, has Utzon been welcomed back by the New South Wales government, at which time he was invited to redesign the interior of the concert hall.

The Sydney Opera House looks very graceful as it floats majestically above the water on the peninsula. With its roof, shaped like sails, sitting on a solid podium, the building is a piece of sculpture displayed in all its splendour on a site surrounded by water. Very few opportunities occur for an architect to be able to design on such a prominent site, and the world is fortunate that, in this case, Jorn Utzon came up with this design scheme.

In 1954, Mr. J. J. Cahill, the Premier of NSW initiated the search for a site for an opera house for NSW. The committee examined 30 sites and finally chose the present one, at Bennelong Point, a promontory enclosing Sydney Cove. It has water on three sides and is considered to be the finest site of any public building. In September 1955, a competition was announced and it attracted architects from all over the world. I was at MIT at that time and one of our class-mates from Germany, named Holtzbauer, entered the competition. The first prize was awarded to a 38-year-old, unknown Danish architect, Jorn Utzon. The jury, one of whom was Eero Saarinen, deliberated over the submissions and finally chose Jorn Utzon .They commented that "the drawings submitted are simple to the point of being diagrammatic. Nevertheless, as we have returned again and again to the study of these drawings, we are convinced that they present a con-cept of an opera house which is capable of being one of the greatest buildings of the world."

It was fortunate that the NSW government chose such an outstanding site, then had the foresight to call a competition, and that the jury had the vision and courage to see the potential of Utzon's sketch. It was also fortunate that the imagination of Utzon was realized in spite of his withdrawal. The prediction of the jury did come true—it is truly one of the greatest buildings in the world.

When the riots started in Hong Kong in 1967, we had some projects to keep us going. One was a switching station and headquarters for Hong Kong Electric on Kennedy Road. The site was in a valley, with a stream running through the middle of the site. Above the valley was a police shooting range that could not be disturbed. The requirement was to accommodate on the site a huge transformer and switching station that would receive the high tension cables from top of the

H.K. Electric, head office and transformer station. (Photo courtesy of P&T Group.)

hill, transform them to lower voltages and distribute power through low-tension cables underground from this building to the city. On top of that, they wanted to locate their head office there.

We set up a design session together with Heinz Rust, the structural engineer, to come up with a design concept. To avoid possible flooding of the site by placing the building in the middle of the valley, we decided to build a bridgelike structure with two huge piers on each side of the valley and to span a huge girder across the valley by resting it on these two piers, leaving the bottom of the valley untouched. The electrical equipment could then be placed within the girder, which would be high and dry above the valley. The low-tension cables could then be directed to the street through the two piers on each end of the girder. Next came the question of a design for the offices. We decided to place them under the girders by suspending them. The valley was then covered over by an open car park where flooding did not matter.

We placed two huge concrete hyperbolic hoods on top of the girders to protect and receive the high-tension wires from the hill above. The external finish was left as off-form concrete and painted with waterproof paint to protect the surface. I felt that this finish best expressed the strength of a switching and transformer station. This is one of my favourite buildings because I feel that this building truly solved a problem in a direct and dramatic way by combining architecture and structure, resulting in an exciting solution.

Another project we undertook during the riots was the Century Tower apartments for Hong Kong Land. The building was situated on May Road, on a tiny but steep site; it had marvellous views in all directions. We decided to try out a circular plan that would take advantage of the panoramic view that was limited by the small site. Two flats were placed on each floor with the master bedroom

Opposite page: Century Tower. (Photo courtesy of P&T Group.)

122

in the front, followed by the living /dining area, then the two other bedrooms, the kitchen and servant's quarters would be at the back. The internal circulation area was short, as it was concentrated closer to the centre. The central core contained the lifts, staircases and other vertical service shafts. There were two floors of parking below the tower, and the driveway circled around the car park to reach the main lobby. The circular shape also took full advantage of the steep site, thus avoiding expensive excavation and retaining walls. These two buildings, the Hong Kong Electric Building and Century Towers, were completed in 1971.

The first time my parents came to visit us in Hong Kong was in April of 1967, when Grandpa Maikawa joined them. They first stopped in Japan to see their relatives and friends before proceeding to Hong Kong. It was in the middle of the riots, which curtailed a lot of their activities. but in a way this was a blessing. Because of the curfew, I frequently stayed home to be with them. We had just finished our new living room addition in Ting Kau and this provided more room for them to stay.

   During their stay, my parents took a trip to Bangkok, Singapore and Indonesia, leaving Grandpa with us in Hong Kong. He wasn't idle in Ting Kau, as he tilled the soil on the hillside above us and planted vegetables, which we were to enjoy for many months after he left. He enjoyed smoking cigars so I bought him a case of cigars, which he treasured; he rationed himself by carefully smoking only half a cigar each day, saving the rest for the next day. He was a hit with the children, who, in their innocence, would playfully mimic his bent back and the missing fingers that he lost at the sawmill back in his youth. He wasn't too impressed with the exotic Chinese food; he preferred a simple bowl of noodles.

13

Starting a family

We were very fortunate that Lana's parents offered us one of the houses on their property in Ting Kau to start our new home. Ting Kau is situated about eleven and a half miles from Central, on the western shore of the New Territories. It was considered remote and was used primarily as a weekend retreat or a home for residents working in Tsuen Wan, the nearest town. For us, however, it was a dream to live in a one-storey bungalow with two bedrooms, with a garden; its location on the side of a hill gave us a commanding a view of the channel between Tsing Yi Island and Ma Wan Island. This view is now dominated by a new bridge to the airport in Lantau.

It was extremely rare, even in the sixties, to live in a house. Land was scarce in Hong Kong and most of the people lived in apartments. In order to avoid any cries of favouritism from the family, I paid half the current market rate as my portion of the rent. It was a small house, but it was flexible so that we could expand it as the family grew. We immediately enhanced the terraces at the front of the house with trellises and beams to give a sense of enclosure. From our

Our first home at Ting Kau, where we raised our family.

bedroom, we built a screened porch with sliding doors leading out to a garden, so that from our bed we could enjoy the feeling of the outdoors. The screen was for the mosquitoes. When Andrew was born, we enclosed the terrace from the dining room to create a *tatami* room and we also enclosed the carport to make this his bedroom.

Just before the riots of 1967, we built a new living room wing, using old bricks from a deserted village, and converted the old living room into our new dining room. We also built a new carport. When the girls were born, we added a second floor, above the old terrace, creating three bedrooms, one for each girl. The house grew to three times its original size. It was our home and we enjoyed living in it. All of the children were born there. We were to live there for 31 years.

Opposite page: Living room in the Ting Kau house.

Lana drove me each day to Tsuen Wan, where I would take a ferry to Central, a half an hour ride, and walk to the office. Lana would then drive to her office on College Road and I would meet her there after work, either to drive home together or to stay and help her in her office. There were regulars taking the same ferry as I did and we soon got to know each other very well.

It was the weekends that we enjoyed the most. Lana's parents still entertained their friends for lunch on Sundays, after church, in their weekend retreat above our house. This house was located at the top of the hill with a pool fed from a stream above. After they sold their property on College Road, they also

moved to Ting Kau; they would often come to have dinner with us, except on Tuesdays, when it was my special weekly treat of spaghetti.

Andrew was born on May 4, 1963. Just before his birth, Lana was still working. Her office, at that time, was located in one of the garage spaces at 7 College Road. When her water broke, she walked to St. Teresa Hospital, which was about three blocks away. Her staff and contractors, who were waiting for her at her office, were totally unaware of her sudden disappearance. I joined her when she called me from the delivery room. After she gave birth, she said I should go to her parents' home to celebrate her father's birthday. As we did not have a name for our son, we decided to honour her father Andrew, by naming our son after him. His Chinese name 安德, *On Duk* in Cantonese, is the Chinese biblical translation of Andrew.

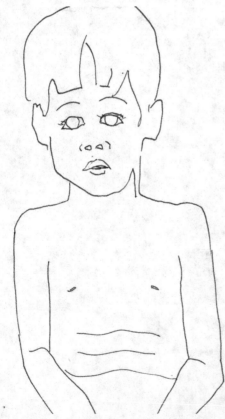

Andrew
28/6/69.

128

Yuri
20/6/69.

Yuri was born on November 29, 1964. After the naming of Andrew, we tried to find names for subsequent offspring by searching for names that, when written in Chinese characters, can be read with sense in Chinese or Japanese. So she was named Yuri, meaning lily and written with the character, 欣美 , and pronounced *Xin Mei* in Chinese. We added Marie as a middle name, in case she did not wish to use her Japanese name. Later, with the fame of the Russian astronaut, Yuri Gargarin, many people mistook her for a male.

Reimi came on December 13, 1967. Her name, Reimi, is written 禮美 and is pronounced *Li Mei* in Chinese, or Reimi in Japanese. It means salutation or courtesy with beauty. Her second name is Elizabeth.

The last, Hiromi, was born on February 18, 1970. Unfortunately, her delivery was a little difficult and suction was used to pull her out, so when she was young, she had a bump on her head. We told her that she had extra brains. Her name, written 弘美 , means wide, broad and beautiful. It is pronounced *Hong Mei* in Chinese and read as Hiromi in Japanese. Her second name is Nicol, as we were expecting a son and planned to name him Nicholas. After Hiromi, Lana found the responsibilities of raising a family to be too great, so she reluctantly gave up her thriving interior design practice to concentrate on the family.

The children all went to Beacon Hill School, with Mr. Cheney as the Principal, for their primary education. We debated at first whether the children should receive a Chinese education as Lana did, or go to an Anglo-Chinese school or to an English school. As we felt that Anglo-Chinese schools are neither here nor there and pure Chinese schools would affect their entering Western universities, we chose to send them to English schools. We now wonder if we made the right choice, as Hong Kong is now part of China and the Chinese language is very important. The children thoroughly enjoyed Beacon Hill School, as Mr. Cheney was an enlightened and outstanding educator.

We joined the Kowloon Tong Club and the children all received their swimming and tennis lessons there. They all excelled in swimming and won many prizes. At one event, one of the mothers complained that Yuri won unfairly because she was mistaken for a boy when she swam without a top. The children also took piano lessons and there were ballet classes for the girls. These activities kept Lana very busy juggling her time driving the children to school from Ting Kau to Kowloon Tong, then to classes for swimming, tennis, piano or ballet, plus acting as cheerleader during their activities. She also had to buy food at Tsuen Wan and look after our numerous dogs and cats, along with caring for the garden, organizing birthday parties and socializing with our friends. It must have felt like a job for Superwoman.

Grandpa Maikawa
24 April, 1967
Hongkong
J. W. Onoshita

131

The family in 1968, at the pavilion above our home. Left to right: JHK, Reimi, Lana, Andrew and Yuri.

I was always interested in sailing but never had the chance to try. Shortly after I got married, I started to crew for other people on their sailing boats at the Royal Hong Kong Yacht Club. Then Ian Campbell sponsored me to join the club. I teamed up with Bill Hsu and C. T. Song to buy an L-class sailboat to join the race every Saturday afternoon. The L-class boat was a small dumpy-looking boat, almost like a lifeboat with a mast. It didn't go very fast, but it was a chance to sail. We raced every Saturday, taking turns at being the skipper. We never won any races, but we did have fun. Every time Bill Hsu was the skipper, some misfortune would happen so we dubbed him Mr. Gloom.

Once, when I was skipping, we were short a crew member, so I recruited Lana to help us out. I can honestly say that you should never take your wife to crew for you if you want a happy marriage. After a few years, we sold the boat, feeling that we'd all had our fill of excitement and that it took time away from the family.

14

Travels in Asia

Both Lana and I shared a keen interest in traveling through Asia, which helped us to understand the artistic and architectural achievements of the past. A year after we got married, we went on a trip to Cambodia to see the famous Angkor Wat. After visiting Singapore, Kuala Lumpur and Bangkok, we flew to Saigon, now known as Ho Chi Minh City. The city's atmosphere was very tense, with tanks and armoured vehicles protecting the American Embassy and key government buildings. It was the period of unrest before Ngo Dinh Diem was killed following a coup the following year.

From there, we flew to Phnom Penh, the capital of Cambodia. We went to the hotel where we had our reservation and tried to communicate in English, but the clerk at the front desk couldn't speak any English. We tried our elementary French, but he still could not understand us as, probably because our French pronunciation was so bad that it was incomprehensible. Lana tried her Mandarin, as he looked Chinese and many Chinese in South East Asia can speak Mandarin. But even that failed. Then, in exasperation, Lana swore in Cantonese, saying "*say lo,*" to which he replied in Cantonese: "Oh, you're Cantonese," which brought smiles of relief all around.

The spread of Cantonese-speakers around the world has been amazing. We encountered them in remote parts of the world such as in Moorea, an island in Tahiti, as well as in Marseilles, and I am sure they exist in every town and city in Canada and America. When we flew to Seam Reap, the French pilot twisted and turned his plane for everyone to get a glimpse of Angkor Wat from the air, which made Lana very airsick. We stayed at a large old dilapidated colonial style hotel in Siem Reap where the plumbing left much to be desired. The food was horrible, so we went into town to eat at the local Chinese restaurants.

Angkor Wat is well known as one of the lost civilizations of the world. Built as a temple in the early 12th Century, in the reign of Suriyavarman II during the height of the Khmer Empire, it became his mausoleum when he died. The complex is a series of courtyards, with each courtyard rising above the other like a terraced pyramid. The outer courtyard is 215 by 187 metres at its base. At the centre of the top courtyard stand five towers, shaped like acorns; the 65-metre-high centre tower symbolizes Mount Meru, the Indian cosmic mountain. It was built entirely of sandstone with no mortise or mortar and, with time and humidity, the colour of the stone has turned dark. The galleries around the courtyards contain vast walls of beautifully carved bas-relief of the *Apsaras* and stories of their lives. Angkor Wat looks majestic and impressive with its size and symmetrical composition. However, I would not say it is beautiful in the same way as the Taj Mahal, for example.

Banteai Srei was a delightful surprise for us. It is a small temple about 15 miles northeast of Angkor Wat. Surrounded by dense jungle, it is modest in its setting, without a platform to elevate its importance. What struck me about this temple were the delicate and exquisite carvings, especially those on the pediments of various entrances. It was first thought that they were done in the 14th Century, but later investigations attribute them to the 10th Century when the Khmer art showed a new lease on life, at the time when Banteai Srei was first constructed. Probably, the most beautiful sculptures and carvings in the Angkor complex come from Banteai Srei.

In the fall of the same year, we visited my auntie, Hisako Obasan, at Kawachi, near Kyoto, in order to introduce Lana to her. Lana was two months pregnant with Andrew, so she was experiencing morning sickness. Although it was only October, she felt so cold that my auntie had to hold her hands while waiting for the train to arrive. It was also Lana's first introduction to *sashimi*, the Japanese raw fish, which was served at my auntie's home. She did not like the slimy texture and quickly swallowed it with *sake*, or Japanese rice wine, to be polite. She has now grown to love it, especially *toro*, the fatty part of tuna fish.

We stayed at their new addition and this was Lana's first experience of

JHK with Uncle and Aunt Yamamoto and family in Kawachi, Japan.

sleeping on the floor on *tatami*. We couldn't sleep very well, as it was very cold with no central heating. We had plenty of heavy blankets piled on top of us and it became very hard to breathe. To this day she prefers to stay in western hotels in Japan and sleep on beds, rather than stay in a *ryokan* and sleep on the floor. Although they are atmospheric, it is too much of an effort to get up from the floor.

Whenever we visit Kyoto, we always go and visit Hisako Obasan. We are very fond of her, with her warm personality and her hearty laugh. Her husband served in the army, in Manchuria, during the war and considers himself lucky to be alive. They blame the government for keeping them ignorant about the true picture of the war. Although their village was spared of any bombing, as it was too remote, the nearby town of Hikone was targeted. My command of Japanese is not very good but is enough to converse with them about simple family matters. When it comes to technical or commercial terms, I am lost and have to have things explained in simple language.

My Japanese exists only because of one or two years of Japanese school in Vancouver before the war and from conversations with my parents. Japanese school was not allowed in the camps. I now wish I was more serious about learning Japanese; it is embarrassing when people speak to me in Japanese because I am mistaken for a native Japanese because of my name. This is especially true when I'm addressed by a non-Japanese who might have lived or studied in Japan and speaks perfect Japanese.

One day, we were nosing around an antique store in Macao, when a small clay figure caught our attention. It was a grey-green celadon glazed figure of a woman holding a baby, and rather crude in execution. The dealer said it was a Sung piece. We never owned a Sung piece and the figure had a certain primitive attraction, so we bought it. A few months later, I was browsing through a book on Thai ceramics when I saw exactly the same piece illustrated. It described this piece as *Sawankalok* and it was used by a pregnant woman who, by breaking the head off, would transfer any misfortune at childbirth to the figure. I immediately studied our piece and sure enough there was a repair on the neck of the figure.

We took the figure, with the book, back to the dealer to show him that he had sold us the piece with false information. He admitted that he did not know what it was and had guessed it to be a Sung piece. This was to be our introduction to Oriental ceramics; we progressed from the *Sawankalok* ware of Thailand and the *Annamese* ware of Vietnam to the export ware of China, which was abundantly available in the Philippines and Indonesia.

We used to visit the Philippines quite often, especially when the children were small. We have some very good friends living there, Betty and Howard Dee. Howard is a deeply religious Catholic who established his own foundation to help the poor and the needy. He later became ambassador to the Vatican during Aquino's presidency. Lana had also visited the Philippines often, when she set up an antique shop in Makati, called Vatina, combining the names of the partners—Vashion, two Bettys, Tina, and Lana. Lana was the only non-Philippino in the partnership, and her role was to supply any pieces from China that she was able to get due to her contacts.

During this time we were able to get many pieces of Philippino furniture and jars for the house. For Christmas of 1965, Howard arranged an expedition to go excavating for Chinese ceramics in one of the provinces. However, I contacted hepatitis, probably from eating something in Hong Kong before the trip and had to cancel the well-planned expedition. It took me two months before I could go back to work, so during my convalescence I started to grow a beard. After I was back in the office for two months, I decided to shave my beard off as it was getting warm and tending a beard is more troublesome than shaving. So one morning when I returned to the office cleanly shaven, my new secretary saw me

Howard Dee and Lana at Corregidor, Philippines.

and screamed as though she saw a naked man. She had never seen me unshaven before I got sick.

Our first trip to China was in 1962 or 1963 when we visited the annual trade fair in Canton (*Guangzhou*) for Lana to do some purchasing for her work. An ordinary tourist was not allowed, so I tagged along with Lana as her assistant in order to obtain a visa. Lana did not need a visa as she travelled with *Wui Heung Jing*, a special document for Hong Kong Chinese to enter China. We took the train to Lowu, went through the Hong Kong Immigration, crossed the open bridge to Shenzhen, went through the temporary shelter housing the Chinese Immigration and then boarded another train to go to Canton, a very lengthy process that was crowded, chaotic and unpleasant. We stayed at the best hotel in town at that time, the Ai Quan Hotel, which still exists today. It is located on the banks of the

Pearl River, and from our window we could watch the hundreds of boats plying up and down the river.

Although we did not do much sightseeing, we did manage to see some sights, such as the five-storey Ming Dynasty Guangzhou Museum and the Sun Yat Sen Memorial Hall. However, Lana could not locate her old Ling Nam University Campus. We later found out that they changed the name of the University. The city did not have a single new building; most of them were pre-war and looked shabby and badly dilapidated. The people wore drab clothes with no colour at all. The women dressed like men, in blue trousers and brown shirts. Everything looked old and worn-out, including the people. What a contrast to the city today, now with modern high-rise buildings, elevated highways and people dressed in colourful clothes. Canton has changed beyond recognition.

We enjoyed wandering through the musty antique stores in Canton. In one shop they showed us some modern Chinese paintings. We selected a few that we liked and agreed upon the prices. Usually the prices of paintings were very reasonable, but the two large pieces were rather expensive. They said it was because they were by Qi Bai Shi and Fu Bao Shi, two of the leading painters in China. We were not familiar with the names of any painters at that time, although we had heard of Qi Bai Shi. We selected the paintings because we liked them. We were told that we would have to get approval from the authorities to take these paintings out of the country. When we got back to Hong Kong, we received word that the painting by Fu Bao Shi was approved but not the one by Qi Bai Shi. In those days, it was possible to get good paintings in China at reasonable prices, but now they are not only expensive but almost impossible to take out.

Our first trip to Beijing was in 1966. We went by train from Canton to Beijing, taking a soft sleeper, a four-berth compartment, and sharing it with an Irish girl who was going home on the trans-Siberian railway. The most annoying thing was the constant blaring of announcements in a sharp, shrill voice over the loudspeaker with martial music screeching between each announcement. It was a big relief when we found there was a control knob with which we promptly turned it off. The trip was quite comfortable with a dining car on the train. I cannot remember whether we spent one or two nights on the train.

In Beijing, we stayed at the overseas foreign guest hotel located next to a hospital. Every morning we could see the hospital staff lined up doing their exercises. The hotel was mostly filled with Japanese businessmen, as they were about the only ones doing business with the Chinese. We would sit at a large round table with others and share the food. Rice was placed in a large pot in the centre of the room and we went to help ourselves.

1966 – Our first trip to Beijing at the start of the Cultural Revolution.

The next morning, we ventured out to the street but could not cross, as a long procession of people marched down the street, blocking all traffic. They were shouting slogans and holding huge portraits of Mao Tse-tung. We didn't know what the occasion was—whether it was Mao's birthday or something else. Then we saw people wearing white dunce hats, with writings on panels on their chests and backs, being paraded by the mob. Everything was upside down. We couldn't go anywhere, as all the roads were blocked. We tried to get a newspaper at the hotel, but all the newspapers were monopolized by the staff. So we tried to go over to see the wall writing but it was so crowded, we couldn't get close. We finally gave up and did not learn until we got back to Hong Kong that the Cultural Revolution had started. Now, everyone was carrying the little red book of Mao's sayings and vigorously shouting slogans and wearing badges picturing Mao on them. These badges soon became collectors' items.

Jardine House. (Photographed by Aaron Chau, courtesy of Perspective Magazine.)

142

15

The Confident Seventies

During the 1970s, Hong Kong developed rapidly as an economic centre. The uncertainty caused by the riots was over, and confidence in Hong Kong had returned. Business was booming and many new buildings were constructed. Palmer and Turner expanded rapidly from a staff of 60 to a staff of over 200.

In June 1970, Hong Kong Land bid successfully for a large piece of reclaimed land for a record price of HKD 258 million. In order to repay the loan for the high cost of the land, the property had to be developed to its maximum potential as quickly as possible. The cost of land has always been high in Hong Kong. It was a basic policy of the government to raise its revenues from land sales, thereby keeping Hong Kong's income taxes low. This resulted in high costs for buying or renting office or residential space, which in turn raised the overall cost of living. Hong Kong is considered to be one of the most expensive cities in the world and this is primarily due to the high cost of property.

The building regulations allow a maximum plot ratio of 1:15 for office space in the central business area; this means that if the land is 1000 square feet,

Jardine House, framed by the Henry Moore sculpture (Photo courtesy of P&T Group.)

you are allowed to build a total building area of 15,000 square feet. However, if you provide open areas on the ground level, for the purpose of easing pedestrian movement and contributing towards public space, you are allowed a bonus plot ratio of up to three, or a total of 18. As this site was detached from the retail centre of Central, we were able to persuade Hong Kong Land to take advantage of this bonus and surrender the ground floor space to create an open plaza. However, when we submitted the scheme to the Building Authority to apply for the extra plot ratio, they argued that the public would not benefit by all that open space because the site was isolated. We argued that we could provide an overhead pedestrian bridge to link this site to Central, initiating the successful use of the overhead bridge network in Central.

With the plot ratio of 18, we were able to design the tallest building in Hong Kong at that time. We could have gone higher if it were not for the arbitrary height restrictions imposed by the planning authorities for reason of flight approach to the Kai Tak airport. These restrictions were later lifted, even before the new airport was started. As Land Co. wanted to build in the shortest time possible, the structural engineers, Mitchell, McFarlane and Partners, from London, recommended using piling rather than caissons for rapid construction of the foundation. This meant that the building had to be designed to be as lightweight as possible. The most effective solution was to have a thin bearing wall on the outside to take the external load and a strong central core to take the internal load, leaving the floor clear of any columns.

The tower was to be 52 storeys high. As the site was away from the main shopping area of Central, it was decided not to have a podium but to provide service facilities, such as restaurants and essential shops, in the basement. This led to the simple tower solution, which exists today.

With the plan settled, the next step was to design the elevation. As I often take my work home for study, Lana interrupted me one evening and remarked that my elevations looked so dull, why not try something different, like circular windows. What a brilliant idea! It would look like a Vasarely painting and I had always appreciated his paintings with their colourful square and circular patterns. Structurally it would make a lot of sense, because circular windows would distribute the stress of the external wall around the building, instead of concentrating it on the corners of the rectangular windows. We made a presentation to Henry Keswick, the chairman of Hong Kong Land and Jardine, showing two schemes—one with conventional rectangular windows and the other with circular windows. Henry Keswick was taken by the innovative design and approved the circular windows, saying, "Why not? We might as well try something different."

During the design development stage, we recommended pre-cast aluminium panels with the circular glass windows integrated into the panels so that they could be clipped onto the façade together. The advantage was that these panels were light and quick to install. However, when the tender price came in, the cost was too high and the Land Co. chose tiles, the cheapest option. It was not a wise choice, and later the tiles started to drop off; this was caused by lack of adhesion of the tiles to the concrete due to the special construction method that was adopted to build faster. Because of this problem, we eventually had to clad the building with panels made of aluminium sheets. This remedial work cost more than the initial cost of pre-cast aluminium, but the Land Co. could now afford it, as they had recouped their initial investment by this time.

This is another example of a building with close integration of structure and architecture. This building, which is now named Jardine House, has attracted a lot of comments from the public who have called it "Swiss Cheese" or "The Building with a Thousand Assholes." I. M. Pei once told me that he was planning to use round windows on one of his buildings, but I had beaten him to it.

Hong Kong Land also asked us to design May Towers, a luxury apartment block

May Towers. (Photo courtesy of P&T Group.)

in the mid-levels, close to Century Towers. As the site had neighbours, we decided to face all the units towards the unobstructed view of the harbour. Each apartment was designed to span one and a half floors, which would overlap. By placing the living rooms, with their balconies, one on top of the other, we were able to produce an elevation that was rich in texture. A new air conditioning system was used and developed into what is now the popular split unit, with the condensers separated from the fan unit. Two units were used to serve two zones—the living zone and the sleeping zone—to conserve power.

Our major work in the educational field was the design of the H K Polytechnic, which is now a university. Our first step was to prepare a master plan that would provide for expansion in the future. We designed a series of circular turrets that served as a vertical circulation system located on a square grid with standard rectangular blocks for classrooms, lecture halls, offices and laboratories, which were "clipped" between the turrets. These turrets were placed on a pedestrian deck above the ground to separate the movement of vehicles from the students. Most of the buildings, with the exception of the turrets, were raised above this deck to give as much freedom of pedestrian movement as possible for the students.

The car park was placed below the pedestrian deck, mechanical services, laboratories, various other service buildings and a large auditorium. Buildings required for for specialized use, such as the library and swimming pool, were designed separately as required by their function. Terracotta-coloured brick tiles were used for the external finish of every building, to give unity to the whole complex. This project can be prominently seen as you exit the central tunnel from Hong Kong to Kowloon.

Heinz Rust found a building site on Sassoon Road in Pokfulam and gathered five of his friends, including myself, to invest in and develop the property. We placed

H. K. Polytechnic. (Photo courtesy of P&T Group.)

12 units of terrace houses in two rows on the steep sloping site and designed the three-storey units as a split level with an inner courtyard. Remo Riva designed the project and Paul Y was the contractor. It received an Honourable Mention in 1979 from the H K Institute of Architects. Each of the investors took two units, so I ended up with two units. As the property prices in Hong Kong rose rapidly, it turned out to be one of the best investments I ever made, thanks to Heinz. We were to make it our home for five years when Lana's family sold their estate in Ting Kau.

In Hong Kong, we had the opportunity to do several large housing projects for the Housing Authority and the Housing Society. One of the more interesting ones was Sui Wo Court in Sha Tin for the Housing Authority. It was to house 15,000 people in 3,500 flats for low-income families. It included a commercial centre, a bus depot, car park, nursery, kindergarten and primary school. We felt

Sui Wo Court. (Photo courtesy of P&T Group.)

that it was important to strengthen the feeling of community spirit within the estate, so the design was focused on this concept.

In order to free the ground level for landscaping, playgrounds and amenities, we developed nine towers, each 36 stories high. Each tower was based on a pinwheel plan with 12 flats per floor, with open staircases and corridors to provide a clear open view to discourage crime and to create a stronger social interaction within the community. The lift lobbies were located on every third floor to save costs and reduce waiting time. Each wing of the pinwheel was placed at a different level allowing the tops to flow with the contour of the site. As the site was divided into two sections at different levels with a public road dividing the two parts, we grouped the towers into three groups of three towers with one of the groups on the upper platform connected to the other site by an overhead bridge to link the community. Therefore one could walk to anyplace on the site

150

by foot without crossing a road and, with a large lift on the lower end of the pedestrian bridge, without climbing steps.

Each group of three towers had their own central garden with a children's playground; each playground was designed with a different theme and colour, so the residents of a group could easily identify themselves to their neighbourhood. The elevation was kept on a simple horizontal and vertical grid, which gave a strong unifying expression; variation was created by the massing and the texturing of the space within the grid. It was to win the HKIA Silver Medal Award in 1981.

Ian Campbell retired in 1978; he sold his beloved house in Shek O and moved to Sydney, Australia, with his wife Zandra. They later moved to London, where Ian passed away in 1994. Zandra has since moved back to Sydney. In 1980 we took in Nick Burns, Remo Riva and Richard Wellby as partners. The next year Malcolm Purvis retired from the partnership just after his wife, Carol, successfully completed her architectural degree at Hong Kong University. They went back to England to retire and, on the way home, traveled through China and published a delightful book called *China Journey*, which included his skilful illustrations.

Just before Ian retired, we purchased three floors of office space in the OTB Building in Wanchai. Before then, our office was in Prince's Building in the middle of Central, where it was convenient for transportation and for meeting clients who had their offices in Central. However, the rent for office space was going up to the point where the rent took a large portion of our operating budget. We therefore made a decision to move out to cheaper premises or to purchase premises that we could afford. When we found that the space in OTB Building was for sale, we decided to go for it, as we had predicted, quite correctly, that rents would keep rising with the economy of Hong Kong. OTB Building became available when their bank ran into some financial difficulties and had to sell some of the space in the building. Fortunately, it was still under construction so we were able to make some changes, such as building a shaft for an open staircase to connect the floors.

When the move was announced, there was a lot of resistance by the staff who had become accustomed to working in Central. They also considered it to be prestigious to work in Central, but after we moved, they adjusted very quickly and found that there was a greater choice of inexpensive places to lunch in Wanchai. We did not have one resignation because of the move. The office is still located in OTB Building. In order to compensate for the inconvenience of working in Wanchai, the firm decided to get a car to take us to see our clients or visit the sites. After looking at several options, we considered a secondhand London taxi, which could be obtained quite cheaply. Malcolm Purvis found that it was much easier to get a brand new taxi because delivery and other services were easily arranged, so we ended up with a new maroon-coloured London taxi. It was to be one of the first London taxis running in Hong Kong.

In 1979, the Hong Kong and Shanghai Bank decided to rebuild their headquarters at No. 1 Queen's Road and invited seven international architects to submit proposals for consideration. We were one of the firms invited, as Palmer and Turner were the original architects for the existing Bank building built in 1929.

In 1929 Palmer and Turner was commissioned to design the best building possible, regardless of the cost. (Even today, it seems this attitude has not changed.) The massing was solid and impressive as a bank should look, graduating from giant steps up to a pyramid at the top, using many of the details seen in the fashionable Egyptian and Art Deco motifs. The two bronze lions on either side of the main door, guarding the flow of money, represented good fortune. Internally, the banking hall had a barrel roof with an elaborately patterned Venetian mosaic, designed by Podorgsky, who was a hard drinking white Russian émigré.

The mosaic was so highly regarded that an effort was made to save it during the rebuilding, but it proved too difficult. It was featured in the news for being the first air-conditioned building in the British Empire.

The other architects that were invited were Foster Associates, YRM International, Yuncken Freeman, Hugh Stubbins, Skidmore Owens and Merrill, and Harry Seidler. The brief called for the new building to be built while still retaining the existing banking hall to continue operations. We submitted a scheme with two towers of uneven height, so that one tower could be built while leaving the existing hall intact. Norman Foster won the competition by designing a building suspended from two sets of columns on each side of the site, leaving the centre portion completely free. Even after the bank decided not to retain the existing banking hall, Foster kept the original idea. The ground floor is an open space, which helped them gain more plot ratio for the rest of the building.

People either love it or hate it. Critics say it looks industrial, like a construction crane, or like an oil derrick. Fans consider it a brilliant concept with superb detailing. I agree with both comments and feel that the concept of spanning across the site does not justify the merits of creating an open space, because the space on the ground floor plaza looks gloomy, like a deserted and empty urban space with no life, no joy and no delight.

16

Expansion Abroad

After our venture into Australia, I met S. P. Tao in the early 1970s. He was to become a great influence my life. S. P. Tao lived in Singapore and had been active in the shipping industry. He fell ill and ended up in bed. While he was recuperating in bed, someone invited him to bid for a site in the central business district of Singapore. He was surprised when he won the tender; this was to be his introduction to property developments. After the building was constructed up to the third floor, the architect presented the elevation of the building to him and asked him to choose a colour scheme. He wasn't too happy with any of the proposed colour schemes and decided to get advice from someone else.

It so happened that he was visiting Hong Kong and asked David Wong, the son of his shipping partner S. S. Wong to suggest a suitable person. I was designing a building on Duddell Street for this group, and David said, "See Jim Kinoshita, a schoolmate from MIT." When I met S. P. Tao for the first time, he looked rather embarrassed when he showed me the drawings and asked me to

Opposite: Shell Tower on the left and Standard Chartered Bank on the right in Singapore. (Photo courtesy of P&T Group.)

advise him on the colour scheme. I looked at the elevation and found it to be an applied façade without any relationship to the structure. I felt that the problem was more fundamental than a colour scheme so I asked whether I could go and see the building before I made a recommendation. He agreed and I think he was a bit relieved at my request, as I was taking this matter seriously.

When I saw the building, I realized that the columns were located away from the external walls and were creating restrictions in the subdivision of the space inside the office. If the columns were placed outside, it would free the office space from any encumbrance and the columns would then be an expression on the exterior and would solve the problem of trying to create interest with a colour scheme. Since the building was already built up to the third floor, I recommended that a transfer beam be introduced on the fourth floor and the columns moved to the external face of the building. I spoke to both the architect and the structural engineer who said it could be done.

S. P. Tao agreed to my proposal, but the architect requested that any demolition work be carried out at night so it wouldn't be too embarrassing for him. Fortunately the architect was very cooperative and the structural engineer did an excellent job of redesigning the structure. S. P. Tao was very pleased with the result and not only did I gain his confidence as an architect, but we also became good friends and partners in other developments. This building was named Shing Kwan House, combining his own and his wife's first names.

After this first project, S. P. Tao became very active in property development, eventually leaving the shipping business altogether. He bought into an old established property company called Singapore Land together with Jardines, using the Shing Kwan House as his asset. We opened our office in Singapore in Shing Kwan House in 1972 under the name of "PAT Pacific." We could not use the name of Palmer and Turner in Singapore as the old remnant of the Singapore firm, which was separate from the one in Hong Kong, was still practicing there.

We tried to talk to Bill Chen, the only remaining partner of Palmer and Turner, Singapore, but it did not change anything. I spent a lot of time traveling back and forth between Hong Kong and Singapore.

When S. P. Tao took over Singapore Land and became its Chairman, he acquired a portfolio of buildings, one of which was just starting construction. It was Clifford Centre and it needed redesigning, but in this case it was too late to do more than improve the arrangement of the car parking and the driveway. Our office moved to this building when it was completed, with our name changed to PAT Architects and later to PT Architects. The firm is known today as P and T Consultants Pte Ltd. (We changed our name so often that we received a warning from the Singapore Institute of Architects.)

The Singapore office was first run by Richard Wellby, who later transferred to Hong Kong, and then by Kerry Hill who left us later to start his own firm in Singapore. He became one of the most successful architects in Asia, developing his own indigenous style of architecture, sympathetic to the culture and climate of the region. After Kerry Hill, Alan Low took over the firm and developed it into a very successful practice. Early on, we hired a young talented Swiss designer, Remo Riva, who had at one time worked for Harry Seidler. For the projects in Singapore, I would first establish the concept of the building and develop the client relationship, and Remo would develop the design. The Shell Tower and the Chartered Bank Building were the fruits of this teamwork. We worked well as a team, but Remo had to leave Singapore and was transferred to our Hong Kong office.

The Shell Tower (pictured on page 154) was built on the old corner site formerly occupied by the John Little Building in Raffles Square. Designed as a simple square tower for maximum efficiency, the windows were recessed to provide shade from the hot tropical sunlight. The ground floor was opened up as an expansive plaza with pools, fountains and landscaping, thus creating a very friendly environment at the corner of Raffles Square. The three-storey high circular glass lobby opened to the plaza, making an attractive entrance to the offices. S. P. Tao established his headquarters in the penthouse of this building. The building was previously called the John Little Building. In order to attract important tenants to the building, Shell Co. was given the naming rights for the building and was the principal tenant.

An old established Singaporean firm was designing the Chartered Bank in Singapore, but they were not making headway in getting approval from the authorities due to a proposed mass transit line running directly under the site. S. P. Tao saw an opportunity in this situation and made a proposal to the Bank that he would prepare a scheme to solve this problem and give them the maximum plot ratio allowed. If he succeeded, Singapore Land would receive a certain portion of the building. If he failed, all the expenses for the attempt would be his. The Chartered Bank, with nothing to lose, accepted this challenge.

I was asked to do the scheme, which I accepted as a challenge. S. P. Tao has an uncanny ability to sense the potential of a site. He sensed correctly that if the government were presented with a scheme where there would be no problem in building the mass transit, he would be able to obtain the maximum plot ratio. My job was to find that solution.

After discussing the problem with the government officials, I found out that the reserve for the mass transit line ran right through the middle of the site and earlier attempts were made to try to get them to realign the route. The solution was to give the government their preferred choice of running it across the middle of the site and to design the building around it. I put the office tower on one side of the reserve, where the foundations were deep enough that it would not be affected by the construction of the mass transit, and I put the low banking hall above the reserve with a long-span structure running across the reserve. This way, we were able to put a high-rise tower on one side with a very impressive low-rise banking hall on the ground floor spanning across the mass transit reserve. The authorities liked it and approved the scheme, also awarding the maximum plot ratio. S. P. Tao won his gamble and we were appointed as the architects.

Consequently, a huge outcry erupted from the former architects, who took the matter to the Singapore Institute of Architects, complaining of professional misconduct. I was called in front of the tribunal and I argued that my client was Singapore Land and was not the Chartered Bank until the scheme was approved. I admitted that, as a matter of courtesy, I should have told the architects of my role. They found me guilty, but I immediately appealed the verdict to the court and won the appeal. This was not the only court case in which I was to become involved during my professional life.

In the early seventies, Howard Baron from Wynncor, the owners of the Hong Kong Hilton, came to us and informed us that the Texans were looking at building a hotel in Bali. They asked us whether or not we would be interested. This was to be our key to work in Indonesia and eventually lead us to open an office in that country. In order to get the feel of Bali, Howard Baron arranged for a famous Batik designer, Iwan Tirtaamidjaya, to accompany Lana and myself to Bali.

The site was at Sanur beach, located on the eastern shore of Bali. After we visited the site in Bali, we wanted to see and study the art and architecture of the rest of Indonesia. We decided to travel by local bus to Jokjakarta as we did not want to wait for the next flight, which was two days later. We later regretted that we did not wait and take the plane. We got to the bus station at 5:00 in the morning to find that the mini-bus was already full. They squeezed us in after removing some chickens and a few goods from the seats, but we were cramped in a crouched position because our legs could not touch the floor which was still packed full of baggage. It was hot and dusty, and the smoke from a very smelly cigarette made of cloves, called *krekit*, was nauseating. Lana wanted to go to the toilet but there was no toilet available, so she hoped be able to go out in nature. There was no natural cover, as every piece of ground was cultivated, and even if there were any shrubs between the paddy fields, there were people everywhere— in the fields, behind the bush, along the road. I just ignored them and did it in nature, but Lana, being modest, did not dare.

The bus kept breaking down and was revived each time by a swift kick to the engine or by juggling some parts, but it finally broke down beyond repair just before Surabaya. Iwan then looked around and hailed an Army jeep and paid them to take us to Surabaya, where we took a local train to Surakarta. The train was packed with people and only Lana was able to get a seat, although it was better than sitting on the bus had been. We finally got into Surakarta and succeeded in locating a hotel, even though it was very late. We were starving since we hadn't eaten all day. The restaurant in the hotel was already closed so we went out to the street to look for a place to eat and succeeded in getting a plate of noodles from a roadside stall. It tasted so good.

Our bedroom had a single bare bulb, which dangled from the ceiling, and there were two iron beds covered with a dirty blanket. The bathroom had no light, so we groped our way around and rinsed ourselves in cold water from the *mandi*, an Indonesian style bathtub. We were so dirty, dusty and sweaty that we braved our way around to wash up, in spite of the cockroaches lurking in the dark. The next day, we checked into a better hotel.

It was worth coming to Surakarta, as Iwan showed us a huge wooden structure with a grass roof that was used by the palace. It became the model for the main reception hall of the new Bali Hyatt that we were to design. The main features of Balinese landscape were the rice terraces that stepped down the mountain and created a powerful image along with the grass-roofed houses that dotted the countryside. Therefore, we selected the theme of the rice terrace for the design of the four-storey unit, with each floor set back from the one below to create

Bali Hyatt Hotel. (Photo courtesy of P&T Group.)

the effect of a rice terrace. We then chose the huge grass-roofed wooden structure that I saw in Surakarta to cover the open-air reception area and the lobby with services located below. The restaurant was also covered with a similar grass-roofed wooden structure but it was enclosed and air-conditioned.

The Balinese authorities had very enlightened controls for developments, restricting all building heights to be no higher than a palm tree and to be a certain distance from the beach. We set the buildings back from the beach and placed the swimming pool and garden in between, thus creating a lush land-scaped environment along the beach. Kerry Hill was in charge of this hotel and he lived on the site as the resident architect during construction. In order to accommodate his family, we bought an adjacent site and built two houses on it,

Lobby of the Bali Hyatt Hotel. (Photo courtesy of P&T Group.)

162

one for Kerry and another for visitors, like myself, who came to visit the site from time to time. We were able to enjoy the use of these houses as a holiday homes for many years after the hotel was finished. We finally sold the adjoining site back to the original owner because maintaining six permanent staff on the site was too much of a headache.

Dale Keller, who also did the Hong Kong Hilton Hotel, was the interior designer. He had a young architect working for him at that time, Ed Tuttle, who later became well known for his design of some exclusive small hotels, the Aman group, for Adrian Zecha. In November of 1973, we attended the grand opening of the Bali Hyatt. It was the first of many new hotels to be built in Bali.

When we were building the hotel, Bali was still unspoiled, with very few tourists. The roads were unpaved and completely dark at night. The monkey dance was performed in its natural surroundings in the village square and we had to make our way along the dark and narrow path to get to the village to see the performance. The dance was very dramatic with the only light source coming from a single torch in the middle of the sea of arms belonging to the bare bodies of the dancers. Bali has since developed into a full-blown tourist destination, and the dance is performed on a stage in the hotel with spotlights on the dancers. The simple, more primitive pleasures are now gone.

In the early seventies, S. P. Tao, joined with three other parties—the Jardine Group; Liem Sioe Liong, who was with a prominent businessman in Indonesia; and Ciputra, an Indonesian contractor and developer—to form Jakarta Land. They had a large piece of land in central Jakarta that they wanted to develop so we did a master plan for them and designed Metropolitan I, the first office tower. We later completed the designs of other buildings on the site. At about the same time, Hong Kong Land joined with Ciputra and some other investors to build the Mandarin Hotel on one of the prominent roundabouts in Jakarta. In September of 1979, we celebrated the opening of the Jakarta Mandarin.

During these years we carried out design work for Bank Central Asia; for Mochtar Riady; for P. T. Metropolitan, which was completed in 1982; for the Bank Negara Indonesia, completed in 1984; as well as for the Indocement Building, completed in 1985. For all of these projects, we did the preliminary architectural designs and the design development, and sketched the working drawings, altogether with a finish schedule and an outline specification in Hong Kong. The detailed architectural working drawings, the structural and mechanical drawings, as well as the supervision, were all done by our Indonesian colleagues, associated with Ciputra. In order to coordinate the work, Kerry Hill moved to Jakarta to open the new office, as the Bali Hyatt was now completed. He would coordinate the work between the two parties, attend the regular site meetings and solve any problems on the site. It proved to be an effective and efficient way of executing the work. However, after a few years, we closed the office; the hassle of keeping an office in Jakarta, with its red tape and regulations, was not worth the trouble. Kerry then moved to Singapore.

We had a brief taste of working in Hawaii with the design of the Royal Hawaiian Center in Waikiki, Honolulu, Hawaii. It all started in the early seventies when a friend of Lana's parents in Hong Kong called Lana up and asked if she could help some visitors from Hawaii who wanted to frame a painting. Lana helped the couple and they never forgot the favour. In 1972, this friend from Hawaii, Hung Wo Ching, was on one of his frequent visits to Hong Kong and encouraged us to enter a design competition for a shopping centre in the heart of Honolulu.

Hung Wo Ching was a prominent businessman in Hawaii, and one of his many positions was as the president of Aloha Airlines. He told us a story of when he was once discriminated from obtaining a seat on Hawaiian Airlines. Angry over his treatment, he decided to start his own airline and, thus, Aloha Airlines

Jakarta Mandarin Hotel. (Photo courtesy of P&T Group.)

The Oriental Hotel in Bangkok. (Photo courtesy of P&T Group.)

was born. Hung Wo Ching was also a trustee of the Bishop Estate, which held in trust all the land owned by the native Hawaiians when they were putting their prime property in Waikiki out for competition. We of course were enthusiastic about trying our luck abroad, so we entered. The trustees liked our scheme the most; it was a low-rise that left most of the palm trees undisturbed on the site. Unfortunately, we were disqualified from the competition because we did not show the underground car park as required under the rules. However, after the prizes were given out, the trustees appointed us as the architects for the project, since they had liked our scheme the best.

We worked together with Howard Wong, the local architect that Hung Wo Ching had recommended. We could not have found a better partner; he was friendly, understanding, helpful, supportive and a gentleman. As we developed

166

the project with Howard, we applied some design features to conform to the many restrictions placed upon the site. For example, open spaces were needed to create a visual see-through effect from the street to the ocean; as a result, the design of the project slowly evolved into a design that was different from the one used for the competition. It still retained the two most important features: that of low-rise height, and respect for the existing palm trees.

The project was completed in 1977, but we did not expand into America. We felt that our future lay with Asia. Palmer and Turner had been in Asia since before the war, and we were now expanding into this area again. We were familiar with the customs, the people and the culture of the diverse societies that make up the Asian region. This was where we decided to concentrate.

Around 1972, Hong Kong Land asked us to design an addition to the renowned Oriental Hotel in Bangkok. I went to the site, which was located on the bank of the Chao Phya, which carried the main river traffic of Bangkok. The original buildings were built with high ceilings and arched colonnades in the colonial style. It was important to keep these buildings, as they were not only charming but had a long history behind them. The best way to preserve these historical buildings was to place the new bedroom extension away from the historical buildings and build it perpendicular to the river, so that all the rooms would have a view of the river. We tilted all the balconies of the rooms on 45-degree angles so that every room had a better view.

A new lobby was created to link the new wing to the old. The old buildings were renovated and converted to functional rooms and suites. Don Ashton, the interior designer, brought many Thai features into the interior. This hotel has been recognized as the leading hotel in the world, mainly for its excellent management, but I think the architecture also has helped. We later designed another hotel for one of the Thai partners of the Oriental Hotel, located further up the river; it is now called the Royal Orchid Hotel. Here, we had more freedom on the site, as it was a not an addition to another building, so we developed a Y-shaped plan, facing the river.

17

Family adventures and misadventures

In June of 1973, Lana took Andrew, Yuri and Reimi to Hawaii. I would join them later as I first had to go to Singapore. They were well looked after by Jean Ariyoshi, the wife of the Governor of Hawaii. The children got their first taste of McDonald's hamburgers and got hooked, which made it easy for Lana to plan their meals.

After I joined them, we flew to Vancouver and took the sky dome train to Jasper, to enjoy the spectacular scenery along the Rockies. After some gentle walks in Jasper, we hired a car and drove to Calgary, stopping by Lake Louise and Banff along the way. From Calgary, we flew to Castlegar, where my father picked us up and drove us to Slocan. I took the family for a hike up to Cahill Lake and we camped there overnight in order to experience the Canadian outdoor life. My brother Kiyo carried most of the bulky equipment, such as the tent and sleeping bags for the children. My sister Aki also accompanied us.

We first took a boat to the mouth of the creek across the lake. Then we hiked uphill following the course of the creek to a small lake. We paused there

Return to Cahill in 1973;
left to right: Reimi, JHK,
Andrew, Yuri, Lana, Aki
and Kiyo.

to rest and to fish. When Reimi caught her first trout, she was so scared that she dropped her pole and yelled for help, which brought Kiyo to her rescue. After another long hike up the mountain, and many assurances that our destination was just over the next ridge, we finally made it to Cahill Lake, located near the summit of mountain. We pitched our tent on the narrow stretch of flat land near the creek. As we only had one tent for the children, the adults slept outdoors in their sleeping bags. The children were impressed when next morning we showed them the fresh footprints of bears near our campsite.

We went to visit Grandpa, who was in a nursing home in Nelson after he had his stroke. The last time I had visited him in Nelson was in February of 1971. When I gripped his hand hard and said goodbye to him then, he smiled at me and said "not yet." He knew he would see me again. This time when I said

170

my farewell, tears came to his eyes and he did not say a word. It was sad to see him so wasted, and unable to move. He used to be so strong and healthy; now he was a shadow of his old self.

We then took the children to Disneyland near Los Angeles. It must have been the hottest summer that year in Los Angeles. It was over 104 degrees Fahrenheit, but very dry. I received a message that Grandpa had passed away on August 4th, so I left the family in Disneyland and flew back to Slocan to attend his funeral. We were very close and I miss him very much.

My parents' second trip to Hong Kong was in October of 1973, when they went to Japan to bury Grandpa's ashes next to his wife in his hometown of Hikone. From Japan, they came to Hong Kong, accompanied by my father's sister, Hisako Obasan and my mother's younger sister, Tomi, who had just lost her husband in Japan and was making preparations to move to Canada. They all stayed in a hotel in town, as we could not accommodate all of them. Nevertheless they came to our house in Ting Kau and prepared a magnificent Japanese meal for us. Fortunately our kitchen was big enough for all of them plus our own cook and Lana. Lana's parents joined us for dinner and got along famously with my parents. They had first met each other in Vancouver when Lana's parents took a round-the-world cruise in 1962. Lana's mother was so confused after the cruise that she thought Shakespeare's birthplace was in New York!

When the children were a little older and able to take care of themselves on a boat, we bought an old junk and anchored it in Hebe Haven. We christened her *Super Tub*. During the summer, we would take *Super Tub* out to Port Shelter, Rocky Harbour or even as far out as Tai Long Wan in Mirs Bay. We would spend a night or two on the boat, and wake up in the calm of the morning sea then brush our teeth with seawater along the side of the boat.

1974, Supertub; left to right: JHK, Yuri, Lana, Hiromi, Reimi and Andrew.

We installed a seawater aquarium at home in order to train the children to snorkel and dive; I made a rule that any fish in the aquarium must be ones that we caught from the sea. So with our nets, we dove near the rocks to catch the fish. The easiest to catch were the clown fish, as they would just hide in the sea anemone and not swim away. Our aquarium soon became stocked with clown fish, sea horses, butterfly fish and many other types of sea creatures, but we later stopped because maintaining a seawater aquarium was too delicate and trouble-some. We later sold the boat as Lana preferred to have a house by the sea rather than a boat, where she ended up doing all the cooking in the galley below.

We started taking the children skiing when they were old enough to enjoy the sport. When the children were still studying in Hong Kong, we took them to

Japan during the Chinese New Year holidays, which usually occurred in February. On our first ski trip to Japan was in 1965, but we did not take Andrew or Yuri, as they were too young.

We first went to Tokyo to stay at the famed Imperial Hotel designed by Frank Lloyd Wright; we wanted to experience it, as it was soon to be torn down. The building was fascinating and resembled a Mayan temple with its heavy use of stone and rich details. Architecturally, it was a gem but unfortunately it was behind the times in its mechanical services, which to my regret, I found out about personally. The heating in the room was with the old-fashioned hot water radiators and we could not turn them off by closing the valves. The room was so hot, that the only way we could cool the room was to open the windows.

The next morning, the room was freezing cold, as they must have shut the heat off during the night. I developed a fever, but as we had made arrangements to go to the ski resort of Akakura, we took the train and I saw a doctor as soon as we checked in. The doctor told me that I had pneumonia and that I must not ski until fully recovered. On my last day there, I tried skiing but I was still too weak, so I stopped.

We were to meet this doctor again a few years later, this time with our respective families. We had kept in touch, and in the early eighties, we received a letter from him saying that he had a kidney problem and that he needed a transplant, but the prospect of getting a donor in Japan was very remote. He had heard that it was possible to get a kidney in China and wanted to see if we could arrange it.

We called a doctor friend who put us in contact with a hospital in Canton and made all the arrangements for the doctor from Japan to come here to receive a transplant. He arrived here and, after receiving dialysis from our doctor friend in Hong Kong, made his way to Canton for the operation. Soon afterwards he called back, saying that he was going back to Japan, as the facilities in

Canton were so dirty that he would rather die of kidney trouble than from infection. We have never heard from him again and do not know whether or not he is still alive.

In 1970, we took the children skiing for the first time in Shiga Heights and combined it with a visit to Expo 70 at Osaka. Whenever we visit Kyoto or Osaka, we go and visit my aunt Hisako Obasan and her family who live in Kawachi, a village near Hikone, an hour's train ride from Kyoto. It is a picturesque village nestled in a narrow valley surrounded by forest, with a stream running right through the centre of the village. My uncle is in the forestry business, cutting the trees for timber and planting new growth where they cut. He was also the head of the local district, which made him an important person in this community. On this trip, when we went to visit Hisako Obasan, we still clearly remember the incident when, to our horror, Reimi, aged two and a half at the time, ran all over the *tatami* floor with her shoes on.

At those days, we found the children were too young to enjoy skiing and they preferred to just play in the snow, so we did not take them skiing again until 1973, and initially only Andrew and Yuri. Otherwise we would not have been able to ski while minding the children all the time. At first we went to Naeba every year, but later changed to Zao and Hokkaido. During Chinese New Year, Naeba was very popular with people from Hong Kong. It had a five-star hotel with a variety of restaurants and was located right at the base of the slopes. However, the slopes were limited, which made it very crowded, and we tended to bump into people all the time.

Many of the skiers were inexperienced, yet they were very daring, shooting down the slopes at high speeds, out of control. Many of our friends were injured by these Kamikaze skiers, even when they were doing nothing more than just standing at the bottom of the slope. The Hong Kong group would monopolize the Chinese restaurant, having one big party after another. Every year the same families would appear to make it an annual reunion. Even today, I believe that this annual invasion by Hong Kong families still occurs at Naeba every Chinese New Year. In 1976, we went to Sapporo with the Hu and the Lim families, enjoying the annual Ice Festival where they competed for the best ice sculpture.

For Easter 1976, Cecile and Lindy Locsin invited our family to their summer house in Puerto Galera in Mindoro, the Philippines. Lindy was the most outstanding architect in the Philippines. He showed his talent when he was young by designing the boldly innovative circular-shaped Chapel of the Holy Sacrifice. From there he went on to design the Church of St. Andrew, the Manila Stock Exchange, the Ayala Museum, the International Convention Centre, the Philippine Pavilion for Expo 70, the Manila Hotel and the Cultural Centre, with which he is usually associated. His talent took him to New York, where he designed the stage sets for Martha Graham.

When Hong Kong Land asked us to design the Mandarin in Manila, we recommended that they appoint Lindy Locsin instead of us. Cecile was more than an enthusiastic collector of Chinese ceramics—she was also a scholar who researched and catalogued the Chinese export pieces excavated in the Philippines. Lindy and Cecile collected many pieces and invited noted scholars, such as John Addis, to help them in their research. Their house in Mindoro was an architectural gem, nestled amongst the trees on a hill surrounding a protected cove. On Easter Sunday they would hold an Easter egg hunt for all the village children, and our children took part. Hiromi, aged six at the time, cried because she couldn't find even one Easter egg, so Cecile gently led her to a special place where she successfully "found" an egg. They had two grand pianos in the living room where Cecile and Lindy would give joint performances.

We returned to Puerto Galera in the summer of 1980 for Hiromi's christening. We asked Cecile and Lindy to be her godparents, so the ceremony was held in Manila and was also attended by the Dees. All three of our girls have god-parents who are Filippinos. Yuri's godparents are Betty and Howard Dee; Reimi's godparents are Betty and Joe Campos, who is Howard's brother-in-law.

After the ceremony we went to Puerto Galera by helicopter, which was the most convenient way to get there. The water around Mindoro is ideal for diving, so we put on our tanks to explore the exotic underwater world of corals and tropical fish. Cecile assigned a diving companion for each person. When Lana was getting out of the water to go on the boat, something grabbed her feet. She panicked, thinking that it was a shark, only to find that it was her diving companion helping her to remove her flippers. For lunch, we landed on a deserted island where Cecile's huge staff set up tables under a huge tent and prepared a feast of barbequed pig complete with forks, knives, crystal glasses and napkins.

I had never before experienced such an extravagant way of life. However, such extravagance has its risks. While on the beach of this deserted island, Cecile handed me a small cloth bag saying, "Here, do you know how to use it?" I looked inside and it contained a pistol. Cecile and Lindy were gourmands, enjoying all the rich food that can adversely affect the heart. Lindy was soon to pass away due to heart failure, a tragedy for someone in the prime of his life and so talented.

The children's secondary schooling was at King George V School in Kowloon. However, Andrew spent only one year in KGV, as he was accepted to go to Winchester College in the UK. Lana and I wanted the best education for the children and we discussed with many people the merits of sending children abroad to boarding school. We felt that the UK would be the best choice for them to continue in the British system of education, with its tradition of boarding in the public schools. We carefully studied the various schools and contacted them for information.

We narrowed the choices down to Eton, Oundle, Marlborough, Winchester, Rugby and Gordonstoun in Scotland. We took Andrew and Yuri to the UK in the summer of 1975 and went to visit each of these schools. Eton was just polite to us. Oundle, Marlborough, Rugby and Gordonstoun were very helpful and all were anxious to take Andrew. We stopped by Winchester to visit the former headmaster of Ben Tao, the son of S. P. Tao, to get his opinion about the various schools. Andrew took an immediate liking to Winchester. We did not seriously consider Winchester as we thought that their academic standards would be too high for Andrew. However, after reviewing all the schools we visited, Mr. Ruth, the housemaster suggested that we try Winchester. We were encouraged by his suggestion and immediately started to prepare Andrew for the special entrance examination required by Winchester. We got Mr. Zaheed to coach him on the subjects that he would be tested on.

Next spring, he took the exams and was accepted. In 1976, I took Andrew to the UK to start his five years at Winchester. Lana was not able to come, as her mother had fallen ill just before we left for London and passed away on September 14th. Lana had a hard time getting flowers for the funeral, as all the flowers were taken up for the memorial service of Mao Tse Tung, who died at about the same time. When I dropped Andrew off at the school, Andrew was so keen on entering the school that he was not at all sad to see me leave. In fact, it was I who suddenly felt lonely as I bid him farewell. To take advantage of my trip to the UK, I met Lana in Rome on September 26 and we visited Paris, Moscow and Leningrad (now St. Petersburg), then saw Andrew during his leave out before we came home.

We wanted to keep the girls at home longer, so Yuri and Reimi went to KGV for their O levels, but we felt that they should take their A levels in the UK to prepare them for university. In July of 1979, we took the girls to visit three schools in the UK: Wycombe Abbey, Cheltenham and St. Mary's Calne. We liked the headmistress, Miss Lancaster, of Wycombe Abbey the best, so Yuri went to

Wycombe Abbey School for her two years of A levels, followed by Reimi three years later. Hiromi left a little earlier to take her O levels at Wycombe Abbey, as all her sisters were already away from home. It turned out that Hiromi enjoyed Wycombe Abbey more than Yuri or Reimi, as she was able to participate more in school activities during her O levels.

Public schools in the UK have three major holidays each year: summer, Christmas and Easter, with leave outs once or twice between the major holidays. They are not allowed to stay on the school premises during the holidays or leave outs, so we had to have someplace they could go to during the holidays, other than the longer holidays when they would fly home. We sought the advice of friends with similar problems and Mona Leong recommended as our guardians, Major Ian and Joselyn McDowell, who used to be stationed in Hong Kong and were now retired in Somerset. The McDowells were so kind to the children; we still are in contact with Joselyn, as Ian passed away in 2001. We were also to discover that their neighbour, Mignon Drake, was an old friend of Lana's. She and Lana had taken the same art class, taught by Chao Shao-An, a famous painter from the Lingnam School. Mignon became an accomplished painter in her own right and now lives in Taunton. She has now turned to pottery to release her creativity.

In order to have a base in London to visit the children, as well as to give them someplace to keep their things during the holidays, we bought a one-bedroom apartment on Pont Street in Knightsbridge, close to Harrods. It was used mainly by Lana who would go to London frequently to see the children during their leave outs. For the longer holidays during summer, Christmas and Easter, they would come home to Hong Kong.

Eupo Air became a familiar name during this period. Lana would often stop by Rome on her way back from London, accompanied by her good friend Dorkas Hu whose children were also studying in the UK. In Rome they would meet up with Evangeline and David Chan who were dealing in antiques in Rome. We still see the Chans every time we go to Rome. Eventually, we sold the flat on Pont Street and bought a two bedroom flat in Cadogan Place, where we still stay every time we go to the UK. We find it so convenient to have a place to stay and to have a base for our trips to Europe. Lana renovated the apartment by improving the bathrooms and entry lobby; she added a fireplace and changed the small kitchen completely by making a huge opening into the dining area.

Near the end of July, we took the family to Bali and stayed at our cottage on Sanur beach. We then flew to Jakarta and took a tiny plane to a small island near Jakarta to go snorkeling. In the shallow waters, we encountered huge Napoleon humphead wrasse and groupers, swimming so close to us that we could almost touch them. They were not afraid of us, just curious. It was a wonderful experience to see nature so close up.

Our idyllic life was shattered when a telegram arrived saying that Lana's father was very sick and we had to go back right away. We immediately flew back to Hong Kong, but it was too late; he had already passed away. We had just celebrated his 84th birthday only two months ago. He passed away just eleven months after Lana's mother's death the previous year.

Around this time, we started to take the children for riding lessons at Beas River. Initially all four of them participated, first riding the ponies and graduating later to horses. The horses were retired racing thoroughbreds, so many of them tended to be high-spirited. Andrew was very good as he had a natural feel for movement, but he started to get bored and quit after a year. The girls continued and did very well in the pony competitions, winning prizes on many occasions. We would drive them every Sunday from Ting Kau over the hill to Sek Kong and along the narrow road to Beas River. They would spend part of the summer attending Pony

JHK riding cross-country.

Camp, a full-time live-in experience for learning not only riding, but also the care of horses.

In the summer of 1979, we took them to a riding establishment just outside of Los Angeles called Foxfield. At first, we took the girls to Beas River and just watched them practice, but later, we thought why not try riding ourselves, instead of doing nothing while waiting for them to finish their lessons. While watching them it looked so easy, but we found out it was hard work and ended up sweating from exhaustion as well as developing sore bottoms and legs. We finally got the hang of it and started to enjoy it. Lana still reminisces about the time she drove to Beas River alone with the tape on full blast, listening to an operatic aria, so she could go riding in the middle of the week without the children. While riding she would forget all about the problems of life. She had to stop riding after she was thrown by a horse and injured her back. I continued riding even after Hiromi left for Wycombe Abbey, taking over her horse, Born Lucky, until she was put to sleep because she broke her leg. It was a sad occasion and since then I have not ridden. Lana says that I'm too old and may break my bones like Born Lucky—except I won't be put to sleep like poor Born Lucky.

18

The productive eighties

The eighties in Hong Kong were a period of great political change. The New Territories, a major part of Hong Kong, was on a lease from China, which would expire in 1997. As 1997 was fast approaching, people were getting concerned about future investment in Hong Kong. Talks were therefore initiated with China to settle the future of Hong Kong. On December 19, 1984, the Sino British Joint Declaration on Hong Kong was signed, which in 1997, would make Hong Kong a Special Administrative Region with a high degree of autonomy. It would be able to retain its freedoms and way of life, including its capitalistic system for 50 years. As Deng Xiao Ping would say, "One country—two systems." This move reassured the investors, and building activity in Hong Kong began to explode.

This was the decade that Chinese entrepreneurs started to take over the old established hongs or large trading companies. These hongs were controlled by a small group of Taipans from Britain but were now being taken over by local Chinese. Li Ka Shing took over Hutchison Whampoa from Douglas Clague. Sir

Opposite: The Landmark. (Photo courtesy of P&T Group.)

Y. K. Pao took over Wheelock Marden after taking over Hong Kong and Kowloon Wharf and Godown Co., from Jardine, earlier on. Because of the danger of takeover in Jardine and Hong Kong Land, the Keswick family devised a clever cross-sharing arrangement that made it difficult for an unwelcome bid to succeed. Hong Kong Land, our major client, was being challenged in bidding for new land in Central, traditionally their stomping ground. The Exchange Square site in the early eighties was the last large site Hong Kong Land acquired in Central.

This was also a period when famous, internationally known architects started to design buildings in Hong Kong. Hong Kong and Shanghai Bank started to rebuild their headquarters with a design by Norman Foster; Hongkong Club also rebuilt their premises with a design by Harry Seidler. Lippo Centre, at Admiralty Centre, was designed by Paul Rudolph and the Bank of China Towers by I. M. Pei and Partners. In the early eighties, there was an international competition for a club on the Peak in Hong Kong. This was won by Zaha M. Hadid, an emerging architect at that time, but now famous with her angular, deconstruction architecture. Unfortunately, it was never built.

Local architects also gained large projects: Pacific Place by Wong and Ouyang, Tai Koo Shing by Wong and Tung, Macao Ferry Centre by Spence Robinson Architects, Repulse Bay Apartments by Anthony Ng and Partners and, on the cultural side, the Hong Kong Cultural Centre by Jose Lei of the Architectural Services Department and the Academy of Performing Arts by Simon Kwan.

After Ian retired, I became the senior partner and became more involved with the administration of the office, leaving little time to get deeply involved with individual projects, except in China. With the increase in staff and with offices in Singapore and Jakarta, I thought it would help me if I took a course in management. In September of 1981, I took a three-month leave of absence and enrolled in the Advanced Management Program at the Harvard Business School; the course was tailored for people in senior positions who wished to round off their management knowledge and skills. It is jokingly called the retread program, for old tires to be retread. It was a three-month live-in program at Harvard.

I was back in Boston, this time going to Harvard instead of MIT. In the residence, 160 of us were divided into groups of 8, called "cans." Each can shared a common spacious living room and each of us had a private room with a shared bathroom between two rooms. The course was taught in the form of case studies; each case was analyzed through lively discussions to arrive at one or more possible solutions or conclusions. Sometimes there were no solutions.

They also offered separate courses about specific aspects of business, such as how to understand and interpret a balance sheet. I took this course, but I still do not fully understand how to read a balance sheet. There would be three case studies per day and you were expected to read them the night before class. I had been out of school for so long that I found it a struggle to concentrate. I often found myself falling asleep while reading the case studies after dinner. The professors were excellent and gave lively demonstrations during the discussions of the cases. Most of the students were Americans, but there were some Europeans, Australians, three Japanese, two Singaporeans and three from Hong Kong but, like myself, they were non-Chinese, originating in America and New Zealand.

Lana came to visit me during the mid-term break and at graduation. For mid-term, we flew to Bermuda to enjoy a bit of sun. At the end of the course, all the wives were invited to participate in some of the case studies we had been taking and it seemed like they all enjoyed it tremendously. The professors claimed they were so smart that they were able to absorb the whole three-month course in three days. We had our graduation ceremonies and a dinner dance on the final day. It was great fun.

When I got back to office, I started to discuss the restructuring of the organization with the partners. The problem was that it was getting too big and difficult to manage from one centre. Also, at just about this time, the Hong Kong Institute of Architects, HKIA, changed their rules, now allowing architectural firms to be incorporated as companies with limited liabilities. Previously, the partners were personally liable without limit, which would continue even after they retired. This was an opportunity to change our organization from a partnership to a limited company and have directors instead of partners. The firm of Palmer and Turner would still exist as the parent of P & T Group, which was made up of P & T limited companies in Hong Kong, Singapore, Indonesia, Australia and Macao. Each office was made a profit centre, but distributions of profit were made from the parent organization. In this way, if even one office suffered from having less work, the director would not suffer as long as the other offices did well. However, if having less work was due to incompetence or negligence, then the allocation of shares for directors would be adjusted at the next review. This helped to limit the liabilities of the directors and gave more control to the individual companies.

Hong Kong Land was a major client of ours. We had done the majority of their commercial buildings, including Prince's Building, Century Tower, Jardine House, Macquarie House in Sydney, the Jakarta Mandarin Hotel and the Oriental hotel in Bangkok. They had just successfully transferred Lane Crawford House from Des Voeux Road to a site on Pedder Street. This gave them a large uninterrupted piece of city block from Queen's Road to Des Voeux Road and from Pedder Street to Ice House Street, with the exception of Central Building on the corner of Queen's Road and Pedder Street and two buildings on the northeast corner of the site, Henry House and the Bank of East Asia.

They had been contemplating the redevelopment of their property in Central even before the recovery of the property market after the riots of 1967.

1978 study tour
of United States
shopping centres.
From left to right:
Bill Powell, Trevor
Bedford and Trevor
Knight.

It was in the middle of the most important business centre, the heart of Hong
Kong. The design had evolved over many years, starting first before the riot of
1967; then it was later under discussion with the Bank of East Asia as to whether
or not they would join in on the total development. After much discussion,
BOEA decided to have its own building, but would have it relate to the overall
plan of Hong Kong Land. As we were also appointed as architects for BOEA, we
were able to accomplish this. The initial concept was to have twin office towers
with a podium of shops and an open plaza in the middle. Circulation for pedestrians was important in order to draw the people across the site, so a diagonal
arcade was created from each corner of the site to lead to the central plaza.

In order to study the new shopping centres that were being developed
all over the states, I traveled to America to study the latest and most successful
shopping centres. I was joined by Trevor Bedford, General Manager of Hong
Kong Land; Bill Powell, Property Manager; and Trevor Knight, Estate Manager.
We traveled to Dallas, Houston, Detroit, Chicago, Kansas City, Denver and San
Francisco to see the latest shopping centres and to talk to and to learn from the

Skylight of the atrium of the Landmark. (Photo courtesy of P&T Group.)

developers and managers of these projects. While in Dallas we tried an unusual dish called "Rocky Mountain Oysters," which tasted a bit tough. I later found out that it was made from the testicles of a bull. From this research into shopping centres was born the present successful system of arcades in the Landmark (pictured on pages 182 and 188).

After this study, we decided to enclose the plaza and make the focal point a three-storey high indoor atrium space. This would solve the problems of hot humid weather and heavy rainfalls and typhoons during the summer months in Hong Kong. Since this was the hub of pedestrian traffic in Central, we connected the complex with overhead pedestrian bridges northward to Alexander House and to Swire House, which was then connected to Jardine House, and eastward to Prince's building and to the Mandarin Hotel. This system of overhead bridges in Central was possible because of the ownership of many of the properties in Central by Hong Kong Land.

The arcade in the basement connected to the new Mass Transit station for convenient access. With twin 44-storey office towers above the shopping arcade, the development generated further pedestrian movement into the site. The total area of the development came to 150,000 square metres. This project received the HKIA Silver Medal in 1982.

In the meantime, the Bank of East Asia (BOEA) asked us to design their building, which was to be built at the same time as the Landmark. Michael Kan was General Manager at that time and we coordinated our work closely with him. Ben Lee was the project architect and was also involved with the design of the building. Some relics from the old building were incorporated into the new building; these included the old granite columns and the vault doors, which are displayed prominently in the banking hall. The shopping arcade on the podium was designed to link up with the Landmark via the lift lobby to the office, located on that floor; this freed the ground floor for the use of the bank. The external granite was selected by Michael Kan, as he liked a Tokyo building that was clad in this stone, so we traced the owners to identify the source of the stone. This was later to become a court case.

Hong Kong Land was successful in a tender of land adjacent to Jardine House and asked us to design for it. A condition of tender asked for a large stock exchange space and a bus depot on the ground floor, which was to be handed to the government during construction of the building. It consisted of two 52-storey office towers and a third tower of 32 storeys, which was added later. In the middle of the site, a low building, called the Forum, was built for a restaurant. The plaza over the bus depot was landscaped and contains sculptures by Henry Moore, a bronze *Kung Fu* sculpture by Ju Ming and bronze buffalos by Dame Frick. This project, now called Exchange Square, was designed by Remo Riva and won the HKIA Silver Medal Award in 1985.

The old Hong Kong Club was another building that was designed by Palmer and Turner; they had completed it in 1897. The building lasted until 1981, when it was demolished; it had become a white elephant, costly to maintain with years of settlement, overstressed concrete, ongoing risk of fire, and kitchens too small to be enlarged. Many members and conservationists tried to save it, but with the high costs of keeping the club going, the confirmation of the building's distressed state and the attractive offer from Hong Kong Land to rebuild the club, a major part of Hong Kong's heritage went. Hong Kong Land agreed to relocate the club at no cost to them during construction, provided that the Land Company was given the right to share the rent accrued from building offices above the club for a certain period of time,

The design was given to Harry Seidler, who at that time was one of seven architects invited to compete for the Hong Kong Bank building. It so happened that the director in charge of the new bank building was the chairman of the Hong Kong Club. We were appointed as the authorized architects to carry out the execution of the project. We were able to steer Harry Seidler through the intricacies of Hong Kong's regulations, which he found restrictive. One of the benefits of being the executive architects is that after many of the items were auctioned off from the old club, there were still many items worthy of saving during the demolition. The superb teak balustrade in my home is one of the items I

190

was able to salvage. I find the new building attractive and the interior space of the club interesting, but opening up the internal space attracts noise, and at times it can be a nuisance at the cost of an attractive and interesting spatial relationship.

In the early eighties, we were asked by the Traffic Department to make a study of how to ease the traffic at mid-levels, where the roads are narrow and limited, causing terrible traffic jams during rush hours. We felt that one way to relieve this situation was to encourage people to walk or to take public transportation instead of taking their car. However, realizing that it would not be too popular to ask people to walk uphill, we started to investigate ways of getting people up to the mid-levels by means of escalators from Central to Conduit Road. We poured over some large-scale maps to find a clear continuous route for pedestrians to take, and we walked up and down these routes to test the viability. We finally came up with several routes for presentation to the government; the closer one to Central starts from Connaught Road, passes Hang Seng Bank to Central Market and Queen's Road and continues up Cockrane Street, crossing Hollywood Road to Shelley Street up to Conduit Road.

The outdoor escalators were to be covered in clear, curved plastic to protect pedestrians against the rain. After we made the proposal, we did not hear anything from the government until several years later, when it was announced that they were going ahead with building escalators up the hill; when we studied the proposal, it was exactly the same as our plan. We never heard anymore from them, nor have they acknowledged that we were the authors of this scheme. The escalator link has become a great success, encouraging restaurants and shops to flourish along its route and to bring a new dimension to its use. It created a new area, called SOHO, meaning south of Hollywood Street, and spawned a series of small restaurants. What started out as a means to relieve traffic has become a traffic generator in itself, albeit pedestrian traffic.

Hillside escalator (Link study). (Photo courtesy of P&T Group.)

We were asked by the government to design the science museum. We were to work together with the consultant, Verner Johnson, who designed the science museum in Boston. He was the one who established a column span suitable for exhibits and advised us on the function of a science museum. Otherwise, we were left to design it from scratch. The site was fairly large and was to accommodate the future Museum of History, which was also completed by Palmer and Turner. We established a grid with a double-column system. The long span would accommodate the exhibits, and the short span would accommodate the mechanical and electrical systems, as well as the circulation system. As there are no beams for the shorter span these services are easily accessible to all parts of the museum.

We created a huge public plaza, elevated above the ground to accommodate the larger exhibits below it and to serve as a link to the future Museum of History. The same grid system was continued there. Therefore, the entrance to the museum is on this elevated platform and is approached by escalators and elevated walkways, which connect to the surrounding pavements across the street. The elevated plaza steps down, at the southern end, to an open plaza at ground level, designed for outdoor performances. The huge steps leading down from the upper plaza act as a seating area for these performances. On the upper plaza, we created a channel of water, which flowed down the steps in an irregular pattern to the lower plaza. From the upper plaza, a pedestrian bridge stretches out beyond the lower plaza and links it to the sidewalks across the streets, at one point descending into a gentle spiral ramp.

The grid system was expressed on the exterior with the columns exposed and with the walls flowing in and out to create movement on the façade and to relate to the exhibits inside. We tried to make the building fun by having various forms project in and out. For example, the cone on the roof reflects the exhibit underneath. I was ably assisted by Bernard Lim, who has since left Palmer and

Hong Kong Science Museum. (Photo courtesy of P&T Group.)

Turner and is now a professor at the Chinese University, and by Douglas Cheung, now living in Vancouver, who developed the playful aspect of the building. I would normally use white as the colour for the buildings, but this being a science building, for the public, I felt that it could be a little more fun and colourful. We asked a colour consultant from France to advise us on the colour of the external surface, and he came up with a lively palette, which we incorporated into the design. This project was finished after I retired and won a HKIA Certificate of Merit in 1990.

Many people ask me what my favourite building in Hong Kong is and I always reply that it is the Bank of China Tower, designed by I. M. Pei. I think it is a marvellous solution for integrating a clear and dynamic structural system into an architectural expression. The concept of carrying the load of the external walls on the four columns on the corners of the square tower, with the use of diagonal cross braces to transfer the load, is clearly expressed on the surface of the building. This design was successful not only from an aesthetic point of view but also from a practical point of view, as it's been claimed that it reduced the quantity of steel by 40 percent.

It has four triangular shafts terminating at different levels, with a 60-degree sloping glass roof. The basic tower is 52 metres square, reaching a height of 315 metres, with an additional 52 metres of height if the twin aerials are included in the calculation. Construction started in April 1985 and it opened in May 1990. It was the highest building outside of North America when it was completed.

The only criticism I have is concerning the base of the building. The ground floor with its vaulted ceiling feels dark and gloomy like the Ming Tombs. With the load concentrated on the four columns, I wonder why I .M. Pei did not express this freedom by opening up the ground floor to the exterior by using glass and letting the excellent gardens on the side of the building flow into the lobby. Although the present design shows a strip of glass at a high level between the tower and the base, it is not obvious that only the four corner columns support the tower. It would have been more expressive to completely glaze the base to proudly show the structural principle of the long span and to bring light into the lobby.

19

Return to China

Palmer and Turner was very active in Shanghai during the 1920s and 1930s, designing landmark buildings such as the Hong Kong and Shanghai Bank Building, the Peace Hotel, the Bank of China and the Chartered Bank Building along the Bund. These buildings still remain along the Bund, preserved by the Chinese authorities. One day, in 1978, S. P. Tao called me and asked if I would like to do some work in China and enthusiastically I said yes. This was to be the beginning of a very challenging and exciting time for me and was an opportunity for the firm to return to China. I always had a fascination for China with its 4000 years of civilization. This was an opportunity worth exploring further.

I have mentioned earlier about how I got to meet S. P. Tao and about the beginning of the Singapore office. S. P. Tao is one of the most interesting people I have met and one of the people who most influenced my life. S. P. Tao was born in a village near Nanjing on Christmas day, 1916, in the year of the dragon. He grew up in Nanjing and Shanghai and considered Nanjing to be his *Heungha* or

Opposite: The Jinling Hotel. (Photo courtesy of P&T Group.)

his place of origin. During the Japanese invasion of China, he went to Burma to join a friend who was already there. He drove a truck from Burma to Kunming, along the famed Burma Road, delivering war supplies to the Kuomintang to fight against the Japanese.

The work was dangerous, not only because of the poor and treacherous roads, but also because of the bombing by the Japanese. During this time, he met and fell in love with Beatrice Liu, the younger sister of his friend and got married in Kunming on May 25, 1942. When the communists came into power in China after the war, he stayed in Burma and started trading in rice, and later started a shipping company together with the Wong family from Hong Kong. His stay in Burma was cut short by the nationalization of all commercial activity in Burma, so he moved to Singapore. At that time, he considered coming to Hong Kong but decided against it. It was in Singapore that we met each other.

He has a younger brother, C. F. Tao, living in Hong Kong, with whom I have had a great deal of involvement through joint investments in America and China. The two brothers worked together very well, with S. P. coming up with the contacts and the concepts—the broad brush approach—and with C. F. following up and quietly working behind the scenes to make the ideas work. When China started to open up in the late seventies the Taos were one of the first families to go back to their village near Nanjing and restore their family tomb.

S. P. Tao and Beatrice have four daughters and one son. Two of the daughters live in Singapore and the other two live in Hong Kong, with the youngest son living in Los Angeles. S. P. Tao is very dedicated to Beatrice—attentive, gentle and considerate to her. Lana often reminds me of his dedication to Beatrice whenever I neglect to please her. It is a difficult act to follow. The family is very close and very supportive of his investment ventures.

Although his home is officially Singapore and he travels with a Singapore passport, he spends a great deal of time in London and in St. Moritz, enjoying the pure fresh air of the mountains. His future plans are to spend more time in China at his house in Shanghai and his penthouse apartment in Nanjing. Although he has residences in Shanghai, Nanjing, Hong Kong, Singapore, London and St. Moritz, he lives quietly and without ostentation. He loves food—Chinese food. He takes his own special cook to prepare Chinese food in St. Moritz. He also loves horseracing and, when in London, and would often invite us to join him at the Grand National or at Ascot or Newbury.

S. P. Tao amazes me with his quick mind. He can work out mathematical calculations, such as cost per square metre of development, immediately in his head, while I am still struggling to remember the initial figures. He can also remember other details, such as the area of land, or the total development cost or the total tonnage of steel used even after a project has long been completed. His mind is always active, even when he is on holiday. He is always in phone contact with the rest of the world. He is daring in his investments and will look at opportunities others would never think about. He has invested in Sri Lanka, and investigated projects in Turkey and Moscow. He likes to lead in his developments rather than join others as a passive investor. He has been invited many times to join in investments in Hong Kong but has preferred to initiate and invest on his own.

S. P. Tao is a patriot and has always wanted to help China. He is a capitalist with a strong belief in a free economy and in business; his roots in China go very deep and beyond ideology. He started a scholarship fund for students from China to study at Harvard Business School for two years. He has many friends in China, but he was unable to contact them during the years of the Cultural Revolution and the reign of Mao. It was not until Deng Xiao Ping emerged as the leader in China that the right moment arrived for him to make a contribution to his country.

S. P. Tao's opportunity came in 1978 when he was invited to invest in

China. China was just emerging from the grip of Mao and the Cultural Revolution. The influence of Deng Xiao Ping with his policy to liberate the economy was starting to take effect. People were no longer afraid to talk to friends from abroad and welcomed new investments in China, especially by overseas Chinese with roots in their village or town. S. P. Tao was more than willing to help, and after careful consideration, he decided to do something in his hometown of Nanjing. After discussions with the Nanjing authorities, it was agreed that it would be a hotel, now called the Jinling Hotel (pictured opposite and on page 196), which was badly needed in Nanjing. Instead of investing, he decided to make a loan and give technical assistance to the project. The site was in a prominent corner in the centre of the city, called Xinjiekou. The project was supported by all the political leaders, from the Governor and the Party Secretary to the Municipal staff of Nanjing, led by Mayor Chen. When we visited Nanjing, we were feted by these people every night and treated like old comrades.

We worked with Professor Liu Guang Hua, the brother of S. P. Tao's wife, Beatrice, and head of Architectural Design and Graduate Programmes at Southeast University (formerly the Central University), together with the members of his staff. His presence helped matters a lot as he understood the culture of China as well as that of the Western world, for he had received his MS in Architecture from Columbia University. He also understood the politics of China and steered us through the various approval procedures, which were very political.

We felt that the hotel, the first modern hotel in China, should be economical in cost and not of a luxury category, which China was not prepared to have at this stage. Therefore, it was to be a three-star hotel with a budget of $40,000 USD per room. This budget allowed the project to have 800 rooms. We also felt that there should be a reflection of the Chinese cultural heritage in the

Opposite: The Jinling Hotel at night.

200

expression of the building. This was accomplished in a subtle way by introducing elements of Chinese forms into the plan of the building. Several schemes were produced and were presented to the mayor. Finally, we presented a scheme with twin towers on a common podium, but we were told by the city's structural engineer that one side of the site used to be a lake and the foundation for one of the towers would be very expensive; thus we quickly decided to put one tower on top of the other. This scheme of a single tower with 37 floors was approved by the client, and we proceeded to prepare the presentation to the planning authorities.

As the drawings were prepared in Hong Kong, we invited six architects from the staff of Southeast University to Hong Kong to help us prepare the presentation drawings. We were also obliged to invite four architects from Beijing, as the scheme was a high-rise and we had to have the blessings of the authorities in Beijing. Their presence was destructive, as we were to later learn that they were sent expressly to discourage us from presenting a high-rise tower. They used all sorts of arguments to reduce the height, even coming up with a different design to argue their case. We were polite at the beginning, but eventually we learned to ignore them and got on with our work. The group from Nanjing was very helpful and contributed greatly towards the presentation. One of them was very good with watercolour renderings, so he prepared the rendering of the architectural perspective of the building.

The presentation to the planning authorities was held in a large hall with about 300 people present. I made the presentation with large drawings displayed all around the room to show plans, elevations and sections, along with a large model and a slide show. Professor Liu was an excellent interpreter for me, as he would not only interpret but would also explain to the audience in familiar terms to make them understand better. There were some very prominent architects from China in the group and it was crucial to get their favourable opinion.

In communist China, every man was considered equal and was expected to give their opinion in groups such as this. Most spoke favourably of the scheme, but the quartet from Beijing raised objections to the height and wanted to cut 10 floors off the top. We were not sure whether the objection was due to political jealousy that Nanjing and not Beijing would be the first to get the highest building in China, or whether it was based on town planning grounds. It is true that the tower would stick out conspicuously in the low-rise landscape of Nanjing at that time, but if you were to look at the scene today the hotel is dwarfed by many higher buildings. C. F. Tao later told me that it was the Governor himself who decided to ignore the objections of Beijing and gave the go-ahead for the 37-storey tower.

The hotel was to be managed by the Chinese themselves. They were not ready to accept a foreign management company coming in to run the hotel. Unfortunately, standards for service and management were nonexistent in China. The legacy of Russian expertise left a lot to be desired. Realizing this discrepancy, S. P. Tao asked Jardine whether the Mandarin Hotel could help with the management and assist in training the key personnel for the new hotel. Soon people from the Mandarin Hotel were flying into Nanjing to help set up a training school and were taking in people to train in housekeeping, front desk service and management at their Excelsior Hotel in Hong Kong. Dale Keller was appointed as the interior designer and did an excellent job of keeping the budget low by encouraging local industries to make the furniture.

Everything was new and we had to start from the source. Chris Ting of Rankin and Hill handled the mechanical and electrical requirements and Levett and Bailey handled the costing aspects. I think this was the beginning of Levett and Bailey's many jobs in China. By this time we had set up our own graphics department, which designed the clever logo for the Jinling Hotel.

I was ably assisted by Ben Lee who quickly polished his rusty Putonghua, the official language of China. We had an excellent interpreter called Xiao Zhang

S.P. Tao and Governor Gu.

or Zhang Xin Sheng, a friendly, good looking and rather tall person. Our paths were to cross many times later as he rose up the ranks to become the assistant manager of this hotel, and later became the mayor of Suzhou. He then left China for two years to take an AMP course at Harvard, followed by a course in urban planning from the Graduate School of Design. He returned to China to become the vice chairman of the National Tourism Administration in Beijing and is now the assistant minister in the Ministry of Education in Beijing.

The first general manager of the new Jinling Hotel was Zhou Hong You, a suave and cultured gentleman from Suzhou, who selected all the original art-work for the public areas. His selections were exceptional; not only did he know many of the artists personally, but he was also a painter himself, so he knew how

204

Jinling Hotel team from left to right: Secretary General Duan, Heinz Rust, Chang Hai Ping, Pat Keller, Remo Riva, Barbara Rust, Mr. Wong, Zhou Hong You, Dale Keller, Lana, JHK, Mr. and Mrs. Tuscher (from the Mandarin Hotel), Edmond.

to make the best selections. It was due to the calibre of people like Zhou Hong You that Jinling Hotel was to establish such a good reputation.

The building contract was awarded to a local construction unit, with the technical assistance of Paul Y Construction Company for equipment and materials. The contract was based on unit rates, which were established by the local building industry and adjusted to the specific conditions. It was not a tender. The project manager was Ian Morgan, who used to be attached to the British Consulate. The project architect was Richard Jones whose cheerful and positive attitude won the respect of the local construction workers. At that stage of development in China it was crucial to emphasize the importance of quality in construction and in finish, which Richard demonstrated by his hands-on methods. The members of the construction team came to Hong Kong to study construction methods and learn about the new equipment. China had remained undeveloped for so long that they were ages behind in keeping up with the latest technology and equipment.

There were no problems on the project technically. The only problem occurred when the provincial government wanted to take over the project from the municipal government who had been acting as the owners before. I don't know the details of this tug-of-war but work stopped on the site for a month before it was resolved. In all my experiences of working in China, the problems that occurred were not technical; they were all political.

On October 4, 1983, the hotel had its grand opening and was received enthusiastically by China. S. P. Tao was hailed as a true son of Nanjing. His reputation was made and so was ours. Through the reputation of Jinling Hotel, we were to receive many other commissions in China. Today the hotel remains essentially the same, but in order to compete with new five-star hotels that are being built in Nanjing, two rooms have been combined to make one large room to upgrade the accommodations in some parts of the hotel. What a change 20 years made in China.

Just before the Jinling Hotel was finished, Dr. Goh Keng Swee, the advisor from Singapore to China on travel and tourism, recommended that to further strengthen the rapidly developing tourist industry in China, hotel management training centres should be established. The first centre was to be built in Nanjing and we were asked to design the centre. Zhou Hong You from Jinling Hotel was to head the centre, so during the design and construction period, he was running two jobs. It was to be a 200-room hotel of international standard, for the purpose of training, and by taking in guests, income was provided for the school. It would have teaching and administrative facilities, as well as dormitories for the students. The site was located just north of Jinling Hotel and was surrounded by three roads. We opened the design to all the architects in the office and Joe Fung came up with a semicircular shape to respond to the three roads surrounding the site and kept it a low-rise building of nine storeys in height. The entrance was from the back, under a circular ballroom at the centre of the site. It is now known as the Central Hotel and is an economical alternative to the Jinling Hotel.

S. P. Tao had an old friend in the Beijing Travel and Tourism Corporation who approached him to look at a site in Beijing next to the Sheraton Great Wall Hotel. I went to take a look at the site and saw great potential for a mixed development. The Liang Ma He development Company was set up with 50-percent ownership by Beijing Travel and Tourist Corporation (BTTC) and the other 50 percent by foreign investors. As S. P. Tao was the Chairman of Singapore Land at that time, he got Singapore Land to take 50 percent of the foreign investment and persuaded me to join S. P. and C. F .to take up the balance of the other 50 percent of the foreign investment. It was my first investment venture into China and, although apprehensive, I was carried away by my enthusiasm and optimism for China and plunged in. Initially George Tso, son of Paul Y Tso, was also an investor but he later pulled out as his family had too many bad memories of China under the communists.

It was agreed that it should be a mixed development of one office tower, a three-star hotel, service apartments and a shopping centre. We all felt that a three-star hotel would be more appropriate than having to compete with the adjacent five-star Sheraton Great Wall Hotel. An added factor was that the latter hotel was partly owned by BTTC, our joint venture partner. We felt it was important to design the whole site, including the Sheraton Great Wall Hotel, as one development.

The design was planned to relate to the axis of the Great Wall Hotel. Perpendicular to this axis, we placed a 100-metre office tower as the focal point for the main axis of the complex. Two identical V-shaped buildings, housing a 500-room three-star hotel and a service apartment, were placed facing each other on top of a two-storey shopping centre; the public areas of the hotel were on the same axis as the Great Wall Hotel. The car park was located under this building. The total building area was 100,000 square metres. Tiles were selected for the external finish, as they were economical and the local builders were familiar with them.

The driving force behind this project was an engineer named Ms. Shen Feng Luan, who looked after the project management of the development and later became the chairman of the company after the development was completed. She was formidable when it came to getting things done and making the right contacts to get approval. Thanks to her contacts and behind-the-scenes lobbying, we were able to get approval for the project without any problem. As in the Jinling Hotel's case, we made the presentation in a huge room with perhaps 300 people from the Beijing municipality and planning authorities and treated them to lunch afterwards. This seems to be the custom in China.

The local consultants were the China Academy of Building Research, led by Professor He Guanqian. They had a strong engineering team and did the structural design for the project. They also sent six or seven members of their architectural team to our office in Hong Kong during the design development stage and we coordinated with them later by meeting in Shekou, a city just across the border from Hong Kong. Richard Jones, now back from his successful tour in Nanjing was the project architect. Ben Lee also assisted me for this project and is now fluent with his Putonghua.

The project was completed satisfactorily and the official opening was held on October 7, 1990. The Asian Games were having their closing ceremonies, and we took the opportunity to attend. As far as the investment was concerned, it couldn't have finished at a worse time. It was just after the June 4, 1989, incident at Tiananmen Square, where protesting students were brutally crushed by the army, so no one was coming to Beijing. There were no tenants for the office tower, no guests for the hotel or for the apartments. It was to take many years before there was sufficient revenue to pay for even the interest on the loan. Today, the investment looks a lot healthier and all the loans are paid off. However, the tax-free period will soon end and taxes will start to eat into our profits. Our investment was carefully monitored by C. F. Tao who kept close touch with Madam Shen when she was the chairman. Since completion, we have added another office tower and are now seeking approval for a third office tower with further parking spaces.

Ronchamps
8/8/87

210

20

The family grows up

After Andrew graduated from Winchester in 1981, he was unsure of what he wanted to be. He even considered taking a year off, as was the custom amongst many of his classmates. Finally, he elected to take a general course, but by the time he had made up his mind and started to apply to various universities, it was already too late. As British university students tend to go right into their chosen careers, he applied to American universities for general studies. After frantically trying to find a university that would accept him at this late date, he was accepted at Gonzaga University, in Spokane, Washington. After studying there for two years, he decided to go for engineering and transferred to Tufts University near Boston, Massachusetts.

After graduating from Tufts, he changed his mind and wanted to study architecture, so he entered the Graduate School of Design at Harvard University, which was headed by Jose Rafael Muneo. Actually, I believe he always wanted to be an architect but as Yuri announced when she was still young that she was going to study to be an architect at Massachusetts Institute of Technology (MIT), he did not want to look like he was following her.

Yuri made up her mind when she was still in high school that she was going to
follow in my footsteps and study at MIT to be an architect. She had a determined mind and all her efforts were directed toward this aim in life. While she
was at Wycombe Abbey, she applied to MIT for early entry and was accepted
immediately. For her graduation present from Wycombe Abbey, we took her on a
tour of Tuscany and Umbria to introduce her to Renaissance architecture and art.
We drove from Pisa to Florence, Ravenna, Urbino, Arrezzo, Cortona, Gubbio,
Assisi, Siena and San Giminiano, covering the highlights of Tuscany and Umbria.
Yuri was very energetic and persuaded us to climb up the leaning tower of Pisa
and Brunelleschi's dome in Florence.

      We returned again to Siena when Yuri went there in 1987 for her summer
studio with her class at MIT. We decided to make it an architectural trip for the
whole family and travel across Europe, depositing Yuri at Siena along the way. I
hired a Volkswagen minibus and drove from London to Portsmouth, then took
a five-hour ferry ride to Cherbourg, travelling through Bayeau, Caen, Mount St.
Michael, Angers and Blois, taking in mainly Gothic architecture along the way.
At Blois we changed our pace and hired bicycles to cycle our way to Chateau de
Chenonceau through the vast field of yellow sunflowers. Then we carried on to
see Corbusier's La Tourette monastery near Lyon. His use of form and space in
concrete to create light, shade and air was original and creative. We went on to
Grenoble, and through the Frejus tunnel to Turin, Verona, and Vicenza, to see
the Palladian architecture, and ended in Venice.

      It was the children's first time in Venice. We stayed in a small hotel called
Hotel Flora near Piazza San Marco. I don't think the rooms were let at all before
us, as the children found a nest of newborn kittens under their bed. The children
enjoyed themselves feeding the pigeons, sipping tea in Piazza San Marco, riding

1987 bicycle trip to Chenonceau. Left to right: Andrew, JHK, Yuri, Reimi, Lana and Hiromi.

the gondola or simply walking along the narrow streets and canals in Venice. We next made a short stop in Florence before depositing Yuri with her classmates in Siena. Her stay coincided with the Palio horse race, something I had always wanted to see. The rest of us turned northwards to Milan and Switzerland to Ronchamps to see Corbusier's church. The impact of Ronchamps in the architectural world at that time was perhaps more dramatic than Frank Gehry's Guggenheim Museum in Bilbao today. They both were so sculptural, free in form and uninhibited by straight lines; both were imaginative and original, but one was designed 50 years earlier than the other.

As both Andrew and Yuri were studying in Cambridge, we bought a terrace house close to Harvard, where Andrew could walk to school. After they graduated, we sold the house at about the same price that we paid. At least they got rent-free accommodation.

In June of 1989, we flew to Boston to attend Yuri's graduation, with a Masters of Architecture from MIT. It was during the graduation ceremony that we learned about the Bloody Sunday at Tiananmen. There were many students from China at MIT who were very concerned about the situation back home.

Venice, 1987

Reimi had loved animals ever since she was a little girl. When we were living in Ting Kau, she would pick up any stray dogs or cats and bring them home. One day, one of our dogs was run over by a car on the highway below our house. When Reimi heard about it, she immediately ran down to the highway and cradled the badly wounded dog. It was bloody all over with its head bashed in and an eyeball hanging out. She bravely took the eyeball and tried to put it back into the socket. She was 12. She made up her mind to become a veterinarian.

Before graduating from Wycombe Abbey, she applied to several universities in the UK. As her acceptance was conditional on her A-level marks, which came out later, I took her to visit universities in Canada and America, just in case she was not accepted to any UK schools. Applying to study veterinarian medicine was highly competitive, and some said that the program could be more difficult to get into than medical school. We found out during the trip that most universities in Canada and America favour, or even restrict admissions to, students from their own regions, which made entrance to these universities extremely difficult. Fortunately, Reimi was accepted at Glasgow University.

As we had heard a great many unfavourable comments about Glasgow, Lana and I went to visit the city to investigate. To our surprise, we found a pleasant Victorian city with none of the slums or crime that we had heard or read about. Apparently, the city cleaned up the slums and tried to improve their image by promoting the arts and the culture of the city. We left reassured by what we saw, but we still could not comprehend their Glaswegian dialect.

When Reimi graduated in 1990, we took the opportunity to tour Scotland with her. We found it to be a gentle and a beautiful country, with fiercely loyal inhabitants. When they found out that Reimi was studying at Glasgow, they would take her to their bosoms as one of them. From Glasgow, we drove to Oban and along the picturesque western shore to Fort William and then to Glenfinnan where the "pretender" Prince Charles had been proclaimed king and had gathered his forces. We then went on to Arisaig, and to Mallaig to rest at Nairn along Loch Ness.

The next day, we visited Castle Craw, a very liveable small castle, and stopped by the battlefield of Culloden where Prince Charles was defeated by the Duke of Cumberland in 1745. That night we stayed in a small hotel in Elie, where a long distance call to Hong Kong cost £138.00! We next drove to Edinburgh where the castle looked better from a distance than it did inside. The following day we drove back to Glasgow via Stirling and stayed at a very nice hotel of sandstone terrace houses called One Devonshire Gardens. We sold Reimi's bicycle for £15.00 and packed her books. Reimi took malaria pills and nearly choked to death when one got stuck in her throat. This was in preparation for her trip to Brazil, which was her graduation present.

The next day we attended Reimi's graduation ceremonies, which started at 11:30 a.m. After lunch with Reimi's friends, the Millars, there was another ceremony by the Royal Society of Veterinary Science. The next day, the three of us drove back to London, in one day, with Reimi's luggage and books.

Hiromi was uncertain of what she wanted to do when she grew up. However, she was very good with languages, so in 1983 the whole family decided to attend a month-long intensive course in French at the Institute de Francais in Villefranche-sur-Mer near Nice. Reimi, accompanied by Lana, had taken this course two years previously to help her French conversation, in order to gain entry into Wycombe Abbey.

Now it was Hiromi's turn to brush up her conversation skills, but this time the whole family tagged along for the fun of it. The course was pretty intensive, starting with breakfast at school, then lessons all day until 5:00 pm, with breaks for lunch and tea. You were not allowed to speak any language, other than

French, once you entered the school premises. If you were caught, and it happened to me quite often, you were fined and the money was collected for the cost of the graduation party at the end of the course. The first day, an exam was given, both written and oral, to place you in the right level. Lana and Yuri got into the top class, followed by Andrew and Reimi, then Hiromi, and finally I was put into the lowest class. At the end of the course they gave a similar test to see how much improvement we had made, and Hiromi got the first prize.

In the mornings, they concentrated on grammar and pronunciation, and in the afternoon, it was more informal with conversations, singing, poetry read-

1983 – Boating on the Nivernais Canal after Villefranche.

ings, and games. They encouraged you to speak up and be confident in yourself, as everybody was in the same situation. I found it to be helpful and enjoyable, especially since I am very poor with languages. I was delinquent in doing my homework, claiming that this was a holiday for me, so the girls did my homework, bless them.

After five o' clock it was free time and the first thing we did was go and buy a freshly baked French baguette. It tasted so good. Why can't other countries make baguettes like the French? The school had some accommodations, but not for a large family like ours; they helped us book a house that was within walking distance from the school. Most evenings, we would cook for ourselves. Weekends were also free so we would take advantage of having a car and go exploring around the country. Nearby were Maeght Museum, Picasso Museum, St. Paul de Vence, Grasse, Gourdon, San Remo, Ventimeglia, St. Tropez and, of course, Nice and Cannes. On one of the long weekends, we drove to Turin to see the Calder exhibition and drove back via Briancon and the Hautes Alpes, stopping to have a picnic lunch alongside a stream.

We got to Villefranche by hiring a Volkswagen minibus in London and driving through Calais to St. Omar after crossing the channel. Stopping at Chalon-sur-Saone and Arles to see the country of Van Gogh, we got to Villefranche in four days. After the French lessons we hired a houseboat on the Nivernais Canal with the thought that it would help us practice our French. We found that our fellow travellers on the canal were all foreigners, mainly English and German, and we didn't get much chance to practice except when shopping for food at the village store or talking to the keeper of the locks.

The houseboat was like an ordinary boat, low and wide with quite spacious accommodations. We piloted the boat ourselves, and if we needed help, it was always close at hand. There were bicycles on board for us to peddle along the canals and go to the nearest market. The most annoying thing was that the toilet constantly got blocked up. Although help was available, he would take hours to come and, as it was happening frequently, we were getting more and more impatient. At each lock, we had to tie the boat down and turn the handle to open or close the locks. It kept us pretty busy, especially when we encountered many locks in one day. It was a wonderful trip, and cruising along the tree lined canals was peaceful and quiet but gave us no practice of our French.

Hiromi made many friends at Wycombe Abbey, and one of them was Christobelle Liao from Hong Kong, the daughter of Donald and Christine Liao. She still remains Hiromi's closest friend. Hiromi applied to several universities but we encouraged her to go to Wellesley College, an all-girls school in a suburb of Boston. As Andrew and Yuri were also studying in the Boston area, it would be convenient for us to visit all of them together. In 1988, she entered Wellesley and graduated in 1992 with a major in Chinese art and language. During one summer, she went to Harbin to study Chinese, sponsored by Wellesley and other American universities. Being totally immersed in Chinese helped her command of the language. She shared a room with a Chinese student so that they could help each other to practice each other's languages.

One day she and her friends were caught riding their bicycles on the pavement. When the police found out that they were only students, they let the girls off easy by asking them to write 100 times, in Chinese, that they would not do this again. During her time in China, she made many new friends with whom she still keeps in close contact.

My parents' third trip to Hong Kong was in October of 1984 when they joined a group tour to visit Japan, Hong Kong and China. Their main purpose was to see China, which was now promoting tourism. When they arrived in Hong Kong, we met them at the airport and took them to their hotel. They did not tell their group leader that they were going to the hotel independently, so the whole group was searching all over the airport trying to locate them until the leader had the sense to call the hotel to find that they had already checked in. During the day, they joined the organized tours, as we did not take them to the more obvious tourist spots on their previous trips, and we saw them in the evenings for dinner.

In 1986, we invited my parents to Hong Kong to celebrate our 25th wedding anniversary. We had already celebrated our anniversary in March, but we decided to celebrate it again in December together with our family and friends. This enabled my parents to spend Christmas with us. As Lana was preparing to meet them at the airport, she received a call from the airline with a garbled message that my father had swallowed his denture and was now in a hospital in Anchorage, Alaska. She asked for the telephone number of the hospital and finally reached my mother. During the flight from Vancouver to Tokyo, my father was eating his steak when suddenly my mother noticed that he was choking; then he turned blue and fainted. The attendant quickly pushed his stomach in and he was able to breathe again. However, they noticed that his denture was missing so they assumed that he had swallowed it. By this time the plane was diverted to Anchorage, as an emergency measure, and they left my parents behind in a hospital. They later discovered that the denture was under the seat, thrown out together with the piece of steak that was stuck in his throat. Lana went through considerable trouble to retrieve their luggage, which had been stored until they arrived a few days later.

For our anniversary, we booked private rooms at the Hong Kong Club and invited our friends for dinner, with a slide show showing pictures of our childhood, youth and marriage. My parents surprised my friends with their dancing skills. Ever since my parents sold their store in Slocan and moved to Vancouver to retire, they kept themselves active by joining bowling teams, playing golf and joining dance classes. When we were young and living in Slocan, my father

Our 25th Wedding Anniversary at the Hong Kong Club. Back row, left to right: Andrew, Hiromi, Lana, JHK, Reimi and Yuri. Front: Father and Mother Kinoshita.

would disapprove of us going to dances, considering them to be decadent. So it was a surprise and a delight to all of us that later he took up dancing and enjoyed it.

We also took them to the races in Shatin. My father loves horseracing and any form of gambling. From Vancouver, they would drive to Reno or fly to Las Vegas to gamble for a couple of days. He doesn't play for high stakes—he just likes the excitement of playing for risk. Even if he were to play Mahjong with his friends, he would insist on playing for money, even if the stakes were very small; otherwise he would say it wasn't fun. Maybe this is a characteristic of the Japanese. The Chinese would go for higher stakes to heighten their excitement.

When the children started to go to the UK for their education, we began skiing in Europe during their holidays, going to Avoriaz, St. Moritz, Courchevel and Zermatt. Then, as they started to go to universities in America, we went skiing in America as well, to places like Vail, Beaver Creek and Park City, where the Winter Olympics were recently held, as well as to Alta and Aspen. Recently we went to Whistler, as it was close to Vancouver.

In 1988, Lana and I decided to celebrate our anniversary at Lech, a ski resort in the Arlberg, Austria; it was highly recommended by a friend in Australia, especially for the famed Hotel Post in the village. We thought it was nostalgic to celebrate our anniversary near St. Anton where we went skiing for our honeymoon. So we booked the Hotel Post in Lech and, from Zurich, we took the train to St. Anton where we were to catch a bus to Lech. However, the road to Lech was blocked off due to an avalanche, so we got stuck in St. Anton. Even the train going in and out of St. Anton was stopped due to the risk of avalanche; the village was in chaos with people who could not leave and who, like us, were stuck there.

We were frantic to find a place to stay, as people were fighting at the front desks of hotels, hoping to get rooms. I stood in the street guarding our luggage as Lana went searching for a room—we felt that being a woman, Lana would have a better chance of winning enough sympathy to get a room. Luckily Lana was able to get a room in a small hotel. We found out later that many people had to sleep in the railway station and in schools because all the hotels were full. That night, a huge avalanche swept over the edge of St. Anton, blowing off the roofs of many houses and killing many people who were trapped inside their cars along the road. Fortunately, many of the homes were evacuated before the avalanche, reducing the number of deaths. The railway was completely blocked and it took several days to clear the tracks. I have never imagined that an avalanche could cause so much damage and have learned to respect the forces of nature.

Reimi was studying at University of Glasgow at this time and was to meet us in Lech, but she got stuck in Zurich until the train started to run. Finally the train came and Reimi joined us. Two days later, the road to Lech was opened to traffic so we finally got through. The whole village was full of talk about the avalanche and stories about people being trapped there.

The Hotel Post was a charming 36-room hotel built in a Tyrolian style. It had a very personal touch to it and was run by the Moosbrugger family. When we first started going there, Grandpa and Grandma Moosbrugger were the hosts, but after the death of Grandpa and his son Franz, who died climbing the Himalaya, their daughter-in-law, Kristl took over running the hotel. Now, Kristl's son Florian, together with his new wife, Sandra, took over the management of the hotel, thus continuing the personal touch of his grandparents. It attracts the country's top chefs and has excellent food. We were so happy staying there that we have gone back to celebrate our anniversary there every year since 1988. We always ask for the same room; that way we feel at home and know exactly where to unpack our clothes. We also started to leave our boots and ski clothes there, which saves us the trouble of lugging heavy suitcases.

The hotel is located in the centre of the village, making it convenient for getting to the ski slopes or to the shops. Lech is a very picturesque village located about a half-hour's bus ride from St. Anton. We usually take the Arlberg Express bus from Zurich airport to Lech, which is much more convenient than taking the train. However, being isolated from the main transportation lines, it is inconvenient when we get snowed under and cannot leave Lech, which has happened two or three times.

The slopes are ideal for us as they cater to skiers of all abilities. They are linked to the next village, Zurs, by a cable car and you can ski back to Lech from Madloch. We go there in mid-March, when the weather can be unpredictable, and in some seasons we have experienced rain and a lack of snow. However, the surface of the snow would freeze during the night and if it snowed lightly during the night, it formed a perfect surface for off-piste skiing, with thin new snow on top of the hard crust of old snow. There are many restaurants scattered all over the slopes so we would plan our day around meeting at a certain restaurant for lunch. We could also ski to St. Anton by taking a free 15-minute ski bus to the edge of the slopes of St. Anton. We would have lunch at our favourite restaurant in St. Christophe, which served spare ribs. We treat our stay in Lech more as a holiday rather than just a skiing trip and we enjoy going back there every year to celebrate our anniversary.

In Hong Kong, the social highlight of the year 1988 was the Philharmonic Ball, where young ladies in white gowns displayed their dancing skills in a re-creation of the Vienna Ball. Dresses were prepared months in advance and many rehearsals were held. Lessons in waltz were encouraged for everybody. From our family, Reimi and Hiromi were selected to attend. There was a flurry of activity, as Reimi got her dress made by my mother in Vancouver, and Hiromi had hers made in Hong Kong. The newly completed Hong Kong Convention and Exhibition Centre was transformed into a glittering Viennese ballroom complete with chandeliers. Sixty debutantes and their escorts were presented to Their Royal Highnesses, Prince and Princess Michael of Kent.

21

HKIA

I joined the Hong Kong Institute of Architects (HKIA) in 1963 and started to take an active interest in their activities, serving as secretary for Alan Fitch when he was president from 1967 to 1968, and taking positions on many other committees, including serving as chair of Internal Affairs. In 1986, Eddie Wong, then the president of HKIA asked me to run for the presidency. There was already another candidate running for the post, but I decided to try, as I was planning to retire from the firm in 1988 and might not get this opportunity again. I had been asked before, but I did not accept because I had felt I could not devote enough of my time to HKIA. I now felt that I was ready.

After a furious campaign, I won by a thin margin and was sworn in as the new president at the annual ball at the end of the year. I soon learned that the position would take a great deal of time, much more than I had anticipated. However, I was strongly supported by the members of the council and by the chairmen of the various committees and especially by the registrar, Maria Lui, who was a veteran in the running of the institute. She guided me through the politics of the institute and shared her knowledge of the members and their strengths and weaknesses. Shortly afterwards, she emigrated to Canada with her children and passed away there after contracting cancer.

Besides looking after the welfare of the members, chairing the monthly council meetings and the quarterly general meetings, and attending the various subcommittees, I also attended many social functions given by other professional institutes, student organizations and universities, as well as traveling overseas to represent the institute at conferences and special events.

In the summer of 1987, we attended a conference with the Architectural Society of China in Beijing. It was primarily to establish a closer relationship between the two institutes and to exchange ideas on registration, education and building regulations. We met many of their senior members, such as President Dai Nian Ci, Zhang Qin Nan, the main coordinators of the conference, Zhang Kai Ji, Liu Kai Ji and Professor Qi Kang from Nanjing. I delivered most of my speeches in English, ably translated by Leo Zee, the most fluent Putonghua speaker in our group. We stayed at the campus of Beijing University and transportion was organized by our hosts. Eva Ho would take the ladies shopping during our conference, confidently stopping the chaotic traffic with her raised arms in order to cross the street.

On the final evening, we hosted a dinner with the menu prepared by Maria and a representative from the architectural society. One of the items selected was deep fried scorpion. Being the host, I had to eat it and much to my surprise, it didn't taste too bad. It was crispy and tasted similar to deep fried baby crabs. I prepared the final thank you speech for myself in Putonghua, guided heavily by Lana, and delivered it to the surprise of our guests. It was the beginning of many interchanges of information between the two institutes.

During that same summer, I attended the Commonwealth Association of Architects (CAA) General Assembly in Brighton followed by the Union of

JHK and Lana with the president, Professor Kenzo Tange, at the inauguration of the Japan Institute of Architects, Nov. 18, 1987.

International Architects (UIA) Congress, combining it with my holiday visit to London. As our son Andrew was studying architecture at the Graduate School of Design at Harvard, and Yuri, our eldest daughter, was studying architecture at MIT, I took them along for the social functions. The only other person attending from Hong Kong was Ronald Poon, who was active in CAA affairs. I found CAA much more interesting as it was a smaller group with shared interests that made meeting and communicating easier. I did not stay in Brighton, but commuted from London, while staying at our flat.

In November of 1987, the Japan Institute of Architects had their inauguration and invited representatives from all the architectural institutes, so Lana and I attended. Previously, there were several professional groups of architects in Japan, which were now incorporated into one organization, with Kenzo Tange, my hero from student days, as the first president. I didn't want to miss this opportunity. We all stayed at the Akasaka Prince Hotel, designed by Tange and where the ceremony was to be held.

Just before the ceremony, we wandered out to the entrance driveway of the hotel and, suddenly, a fleet of cars with tight security drove up. A row of kimono-clad women lined up along the driveway. The main car stopped and out came the princess, who then stood by the open door until Crown Prince Akihito came out. As he emerged, everyone bowed, including the princess, and then followed him into the hotel. It seemed strange that even his wife had to bow to him.

They were the guests of honour at the ceremony and, afterwards, went around mixing with the guests. When they came to us, Lana explained that she came from Hong Kong, and I added that I lived in Hong Kong but was born in Canada from Japanese parents. The Princess then asked, in excellent English, how my parents were. I felt very touched by her interest.

That evening, Kenzo Tange and his wife hosted a dinner party with Mr. Brewster, president of the AIA, and his wife; Richard Rogers from the UK; Dudley from Australia; Yang Soon Suan from Singapore and others as guests. Mrs. Tange turned out to be a very elegant hostess, vivacious and charming, who seemed to know everybody who was somebody in Japan. She was much livelier than Tange, who was very quiet and reserved and definitely not the gregarious type.

During my visit to Japan, an architectural competition, sponsored by the government, the Royal HK Jockey Club and HKIA, for a new University of Science and Technology was being judged. One of the external juror members invited by the HKIA was Fumihiko Maki from Japan. What happened was extraordinary. The jury selected Professor Eric Lye together with Wong and Ouyang as

228

Spring Dinner March 1988

The Hong Kong Institute of Architects

香港建築師學會

HKIA council with past presidents.

the winners and presented the prize money, but the University Board then awarded the commission to Simon Kwan together with John Harris as it was rumoured
that the new president of the university preferred the latter's design, especially for
the entrance to the university.

I was caught in a dilemma as to whether or not the institute should object
to this unseemly action. I did not take any action, since the act was not against
the rules and there was nothing we could do. However as I reflect upon this
event, I now feel that I should have at least voiced our disapproval of the extraordinary action, even if it was not against the rules.

HKIA skit at the 1988 Arcasia Congress in Seoul, Korea.

In November of 1988, we attended the Ninth Arcasia Council Meeting in Seoul, Korea. Arcasia is an organization of architects in the Asian Region, which was formed to exchange information and assist each other in the promotion of architecture in Asia. I met many of the members before through CAA, where Singapore, Malaysia, India, Pakistan and Sri Lanka were represented. Like CAA, the group was small enough to get to know most members, which made

JHK with Patrick Lau and the Governor, Sir David Wilson.

the event friendly, rewarding and interesting. Besides representatives from Asia, the Brewsters from AIA and Rod Hackney from RIBA (Royal Institute of British Architects) were also invited. We had a strong group of ten people from HKIA.

At the closing dinner members of each institute had to sing their country's national song. As Hong Kong had no national anthem, we were stuck as to what we should sing. We finally chose "Descendants of the Dragon" to symbolize our roots in China since it had a rousing tune. This was before 1997, but I am sure that China would approve, as they were not members of Arcasia in 1988. After the conference, there were organized tours of Seoul and Kyongju, which we joined. I was amazed at the similarity of their architecture to that of the Japanese.

Also in November, the governor, Sir David Wilson came to open our annual award exhibition at the Landmark. At our annual ball, I passed the presidency on to Christopher Haffner. It was a rich and rewarding experience, a fitting end to my active professional life.

22

Retirement

In 1988, I retired from Palmer and Turner after 28 years with the firm. It had been a custom in Palmer and Turner for partners to retire at 55, and although there was no written rule that said one must retire at 55, I felt that I should continue with the tradition, as many of the younger partners would anticipate this and look forward to taking up greater responsibilities. Heinz Rust also retired in the same year. Notices were sent to our friends and clients to make the announcement, and a cocktail party was held at the Hong Kong Club on September 30 to bid us adieu.

The first few weeks after retirement, I felt a little strange, with an empty feeling, not going to the office every morning. I was totally unprepared for a life of retirement. I first thought that this was the end of life for me—being idle with no purpose in life. On the other hand, I could look at it as an opportunity to do something else, to start a new life completely different from my previous way of life. Perhaps I could take up artwork again, go back to creating my sculptures, or try Chinese painting, as I admired many of the 20th-century Chinese paintings.

However, I was soon caught up with ongoing commitments that kept me busy and, with new situations emerging, I drifted into the future.

It was during this time of uncertainty that S. P. Tao asked me to consult on his Singapore Land projects in Russia and Turkey, and I was happy to accept. In October of 1989, S. P. Tao and I flew to Moscow and met up with the people from Melodia, a record company, who were seeking partners for investment in a hotel. We were shown two or three sites for consideration, but I felt that none of them was suitable as they were all too far from Red Square. Land in the centre of Moscow was at a premium, even in those days, so we decided not to pursue this investment any further. However, I must say that S. P. Tao was very forward thinking to have considered investing in Moscow, before Perestroika.

The second investment we looked at was in Ankara, Turkey, when we visited there in December, before returning to Hong Kong just before Christmas. The Turkish developers were a group of brothers of the Aymet family. They needed a foreign investor to inject US dollars into their project in order to make it go. They owned quite a few properties in Ankara and Istanbul that we took a look at, but their immediate project was a hotel site in Ankara. The location of the site was quite good, but the shape of the site was not ideal. It was wedge shaped, with the pointed end facing the road, giving a narrow frontage, but as there were no other high-rises nearby, the rooms would have unobstructed views all around, even to the presidential palace. They already had an architect selected for the project.

Singapore Land had signed an agreement to enter into a joint venture called Aymet Singapore Land Turizm A.S. We did a preliminary concept for the project, as did their architect. Finally it ended up as a compromise between the two schemes, taking the best of both, which was a diplomatic solution. It took a long time to develop the site, but I believe that Singapore Land is still involved in this recently completed hotel. We visited Istanbul again in July of 1990, this time to see their sites in Istanbul, but since the land was involved politically, the Istanbul project never materialized.

About this time, Singapore Land became involved with a landlord from Thailand who wanted to build a shopping centre on a huge piece of property he owned in the middle of Bangkok. S. P. Tao called me and we worked out an itinerary to travel together, along with this landlord, to visit various shopping centres around the world . Our first stop was Brussels where Peter Rogowski, the joint managing partner from Trammel Crow International, joined us. It was then on to Paris where we visited the still incomplete glass pyramid of the Louvre, as arranged by I. M. Pei. From Paris, we went to Montreal, Toronto and Edmonton to see their latest shopping centres, especially the one in Edmonton, as it was the biggest shopping centre and incorporated entertainment—a new concept. We chose the Canadian examples because their cold climate had encouraged them to design climate-controlled environments; these ideas could be applied equally to the hot and humid climate of Bangkok.

San Antonio, our next stop, was a delight. The city took advantage of the river that flows through the middle of the city to create the main link and is the driving force for movement of people. The waterway was improved with parks, shops and restaurants dotted along the shore with a boat service running along the river. New developments were built along this river, creating waterways into the buildings and linking them to the rest of the city. It is truly a pleasure to stroll along the river and enjoy the view, as well as to shop or stop to have a bite. It is one of the most successful urbanization schemes developed in America. We felt that Thailand with its myriads of canals could develop a similar theme. The project, however, did not go ahead, as the landlord decided to go with another group, but I do hope that Bangkok will follow the example of San Antonio and develop the rich potential of her waterways.

One day, not long after my retirement, someone from Kuok Bros. called me up and asked whether I would be interested in helping them design an office building. I went to their office and accepted a commission to do the design and the preliminary drawings for an office building in Kowloon Bay. The Kuok Bros. organization, led by Robert Kuok, owned the Shangri-La Hotels and a great many housing and commercial developments, especially in China. They had an in-house architectural team who carried out the working drawings and the supervision. I teamed up with Ben Lee who had also left Palmer and Turner at the same time as I did. As we did not have an office to do the work, we used the office of H. Y. Chan, a former employee of P & T; his office was conveniently located on Kennedy Road.

The Kowloon Bay area had a height limit, due to its proximity to the airport. In order to maximize the floor area, the design ended up in an X-shape with a sky lobby on the second floor, and with long escalators on the external façade, leading to the lobby from the ground level. The result was quite successful, both for its design and as a business venture.

23

Tao and Kinoshita

In 1990, S. P. Tao suggested that we get together and form a consulting firm to carry out projects in administration, finance and design. He would look after the setting up of a project management team and the financing for the project and I would look after the design. We were to name this organization "Tao and Kinoshita, Consultants." The projects we handled were all his own investments, namely, the twin tower World Trade Centre in Colombo, the huge Shanghai Trade Mart, the later phase of the Liang Ma He Project in Beijing and the Suzhou Garden Villa for his brother, C. F. Tao. I got Ben Lee to assist me as a consultant, and we established an office on the 66th floor of the Bank of China Tower.

The project in Colombo, Sri Lanka, formerly Ceylon, was mainly funded by S. P. Tao. He had a long association with Sri Lanka from his earlier days in shipping and was well connected with the people in the government and in business circles. The project is listed on the Colombo stock exchange, but S. P. Tao owns most of the shares. The site had been taken over from HSBC, who had a lien on it from the bankrupt Overseas Trust Bank. The site was in a prime location, right in the middle of Colombo's business district and next to the Hilton Hotel, where it was convenient for us to stay on our numerous trips to Colombo.

S. P. Tao wanted two buildings, one to keep and the other to sell, so we designed a twin tower complex with a common podium. The two towers were identical, each square with semicircular corners facing each other. The main lift lobby was on the second floor, with a skylight above, creating a light and spacious atrium space. Below it was the commercial space, with car parking behind it and continuing into the basement. Cars could gain access at the back of the second floor lobby by driving up a gentle ramp from each side of the podium. At 34 stories, it was the highest building in Colombo and probably will remain so for some time.

After we completed the preliminary drawings, we appointed Anthony Ng of Hong Kong as the architects, as they had been the architects for the original project on the same site for OTB; we therefore reasoned that they would be familiar with the conditions in Sri Lanka. To manage the project, S. P. Tao brought in Martin Pereira from Singapore, who turned out to be an excellent project manager. For the resident architect, Ben Lee went to the UK to interview several respondents to an advertisement and selected Ian Jennings, who also proved to be an excellent choice. After Ian finished the project, he worked in Hong Kong for Anthony Ng, but he later returned to Sri Lanka, making it his home.

It was a good team and we all enjoyed working together. The general contract was negotiated with Turner Steiner East Asia Ltd. with Bob McAllister looking after the day-to-day affairs. The most contentious issue that came up concerned the structural system. When Turner was given the drawings to negotiate a price, they came back with a pre-cast façade for the entire project, which they claimed would save time and money. This meant that the structural system had to be redesigned entirely and Turner was prepared to absorb the cost, so the

Opposite: World Trade Centre, Columbo.

structural engineers were changed to their engineers.

The change to a pre-cast façade remained a thorny issue and the architects, Anthony Ng, would not approve the details of the joints for the pre-cast panels, as proposed by Turner. A factory for the pre-cast panels was set up on the outskirts of Colombo, and soon we were delivering the panels to the site. Strict controls on the quality and the colour of the aggregate were maintained throughout the construction. We persuaded Ena da Silva, a well-known local artist, to contribute something for the lobby. She suggested a series of light metal sculptures, floating in the space of the lobby, designed by one of her protégés.

The project was completed and the president of Sri Lanka, Kumaratunga, came to officiate at the opening. Security was tight. She arrived in a cavalcade of six identical cars so no one would know which car she was in. In the lobby, while they were officiating, Lana wanted to go to the washroom and started to move away from the crowd. Immediately a guard was upon her and followed her, asking where she was going. All went well with the speeches, the traditional dancing and the cocktails that followed. However, three days after we left Colombo, Lana was watching the news on television and saw that a bomb blast had destroyed part of the World Trade Centre in Colombo.

I immediately telephoned S. P. Tao to confirm the news. We had to return right away to assess the damage and take remedial measures. The bomb went off at the back of the building, shattering 70 percent of the windows on the two towers; it had completely destroyed one of the columns in the now badly damaged car park at the rear of the building. It took one year to bring the building back to its original condition; in addition some areas, such as the mullions to the glass curtain wall in the podium, were strengthened.

This was not the only time the Tamil Tigers released bombs in the city. About a year earlier, a nearby bank building had been almost completely destroyed and many neighbouring buildings damaged, including ours. However,

240

for us the damage had not been as severe as it was this time at the World Trade Centre. Because of this conflict, the whole economy of Sri Lanka was affected, creating a strained business environment. We hope that the latest round of talks will be successful in bring lasting peace and a solution to this conflict.

S. P. Tao always wanted to build a trade mart similar to the ones Trammel Crow did in Dallas and John Portman built in Atlanta. An opportunity arose in Shanghai, a city he was familiar with. He sensed that, in the future, Shanghai would be the centre of trade and manufacturing in China and a trade mart was the right vehicle for promoting this trade—a one-stop mart where a buyer could source his supply, get all the necessary approvals, such as customs clearance, and ship to wherever he wanted—all under one roof. S. P. took 25 percentof the equity; another 25 percent was taken by an Indonesian friend, Liem Sioe Liong, and the other 50 percent by two Taiwanese friends.

A huge site was identified near the Hongqiao Airport in the western part of Shanghai. For the project management, S. P. got his nephew, Chau Jia Long, to live in Shanghai and monitor the project. He was the ideal person for the project; he understood the Chinese way of thinking and he had the ability to negotiate with the contractors on the cost. The total size of the built-up area would be over three million square feet and the total cost would be under $270 million USD.

The architects for the project were ECADI—East China Architectural Design Institute. In order to acquaint them with the workings of a mart, we took their designers to Dallas and to Brussels to show them Trammell Crow's marts, and to Atlanta to show them John Portman's mart. We laid out the requirements for the mart with the help of Gus Dubinski and Peter Rogowski, of Trammel Crow International in Brussels. The design was done by ECADI with us guiding them through the functional aspects of the design. Several of their model makers went to Atlanta to develop a better technique of making models by working together with John Portman's people.

The project was not without its share of problems, but these were of a political nature, such as a misunderstanding with the Chinese partners on the terms of the agreement, which at one time stopped construction for a short while. We never had any problems technically. In the end all was well and the project was completed to everyone's satisfaction. We had no problems with ECADI as architects, nor with the structural, mechanical or electrical engineers, who all performed in a very professional way. The attitude of key people, such as the vice-mayor of Shanghai, played a very important role in the success of a project in Shanghai. I suppose this would apply elsewhere, but probably more so in China where personal contact plays such an important part in business.

The project in Liang Ma He, also known as Landmark in English, started when I was still with Palmer and Turner and was covered in the chapter "Return to China." After the completion of this project, C. F. Tao became the deputy chairman of the company and started to look into further expansion of the development. So we did a series of schemes for possible extensions and subsequently built an additional office tower on the site. We are still considering building another tower but this has been delayed until we fulfill the requirements for car parking spaces for that development.

When we first built the project, there were not that many cars around, so many of the available car park spaces were used for storage and as service areas. Recently there has been a sudden increase in the number of cars and the site is overcrowded with them. Now, not only do the former spaces for cars have to be reinstated, but more parking stalls have to be built to complement additional office space; this places a limitation on the use of the remaining land. This will become a universal problem throughout China as the number of cars increase.

The Suzhou Garden Villa was mainly a project of S. P. Tao's brother, C. F. Tao, with S. P. holding a share. This was started when Zhang Xin Shang was still the mayor of Suzhou, and he had encouraged C. F. to invest. He obtained some land in the western part of Suzhou in the New District. Suzhou has a very good policy for her future development. They decided to restore and rejuvenate the old central part of the city, thus preserving its character, and any new development is permitted outside the city walls, namely in the New District, to the west; the new development with the Singapore government is similarly limited to the east of the old city.

C. F. asked me to develop a master plan for the site. He wanted to create a community for overseas Chinese who wanted to retire or to have a second home in Suzhou, and for expatriates who would be coming to Suzhou to set up factories and other businesses. Therefore, it was to be a mix of houses and apartments with a central sports and recreational facility, as well as a small supermarket and a coffee shop. When I think about Suzhou, there are three strong characteristics that make it unique from any other city in China. They are her waterways or canals, the famed Suzhou gardens, and the black roofs and white walls of the houses. With these three images in mind, I designed the individual houses in the black and white Suzhou motif, with gardens around them, and located them along a canal. Anyone living here would not think that he is living anywhere else but Suzhou.

The major part of the site was devoted to these individual houses with the high-rise apartments situated closer to the amenities. A disused canal ran that across the middle of the site was brought to life by surrounding it with gardens and terraces and extending the canal to the individual houses. Nelson Chen was appointed as the architect to carry out the project, and it is now completed, with the exception of some of the houses at the back of the property.

I started to take Mandarin lessons in the early eighties when we started to get involved with projects in China, but no matter how hard I try, I never seem to improve or get beyond the point where I can only vaguely understand what people are saying. I have learned to say a few phrases, but I am hopeless at understanding the responses. However, I was able to give a short speech in Mandarin at a dinner in Beijing, given by HKIA; Lana assisted me in the preparation and I rehearsed before the event. I gave up taking lessons in 1990 when my Chinese teacher immigrated to the USA. Now I seem to have forgotten everything. My capacity for learning languages is very poor and seems to get worse as I get older. I feel very ashamed of myself because I still cannot speak or understand Cantonese after living in Hong Kong for over 40 years.

In September of 2000, when the lease with the Bank of China expired and a higher rent was demanded, we closed the office of Tao and Kinoshita, Consultants. Our work on the Shanghai Mart was finished and there was no other work in sight. However, the firm still exists and I am still involved with projects that S. P. Tao initiated, such as his mixed development in Colombo, Sri Lanka, which he started in 2003.

24

The Bank of East Asia case

An unexpected and unpleasant event arose during this period of my life. In 1983, during my time with Palmer and Turner, we completed the headquarters for the Bank of East Asia. For the external cladding, we used a grey granite, which later started to fall off. Therefore the Bank sued both the stone contractor, Tsien Wui Marble Factory Limited, and the four partners of Palmer and Turner from that time: myself, Heinz Rust, Nick Burns and Remo Riva.

At this stage of life it was the last thing I could have wished for—to be involved in a court case after I had been retired for eight years. I received the writ on July 17, 1996, but I knew earlier that the writ would be coming. About a month before, a reporter called me up and asked me about the writ that was issued from Bank of East Asia or BOEA. I told him I knew nothing about it and he explained what the writ was about. How he knew the details I have no idea, but it was a warning to expect the writ. I called up Heinz Rust and Nick Burns, but both were away in Europe. Remo, too, was not around. I then got a call from Malcolm Purvis in England, who said that he'd gotten a call from Nick Burns in

Ireland about the writ; I told Malcolm that his name was not on the writ.

Nick Burns already had Geoffrey Shaw of McKenna Minter Ellison as his lawyer for the case, so Heinz and I decided to go along with it. In hindsight, we should have done a much more thorough investigation before selecting our lawyer. Just to be on the safe side, I asked Anthony Poon of Baker and McKenzie to look after my interests, with the understanding that I did not wish to do anything that would hurt my former partners.

The court case started near the end of May, and I was called to give evidence as the partner in charge at that time. I was followed by Ben Lee, who was the project architect, and Peter Tse, who was the project engineer. Jonathan Harris was our barrister and Mr. Justice Findlay was the judge. We argued that the design for fixing the granite was done by the contractors and, therefore, they were responsible. Nonetheless, it was past the statute of limitations in any case. As we were unfamiliar with the dry fixing method of installing granite, we sent it out for tender, stating that the tenderer had to provide the fixing details as well as the price. Near the end of the hearing, our barrister felt that in order to gain the sympathy of the judge, it would be better to admit to one of the charges, namely that we were in breach of our duty of care that we owed to the bank. Later, all the other lawyers said that we should never have made that admittance.

On June 25, 1997, a few days before Hong Kong reverted back to China, the judgement came—it was awarded to the bank. The damages came to $38,503,000 Hong Kong dollars, with interest for each day we delayed. As I had the most shares during the construction of the bank, my portion of the damages was the highest. However, the firm of Palmer and Turner had to share in the liability. Before the judgement came out, it was discovered that when we changed from a partnership to a corporation in 1982, there was a clause whereby all partners giving up their partnership shares would be protected from any liability before this date. This meant that the new company of Palmer and Turner Ltd.

246

was responsible for any liability incurred by the partners. However, this had to be interpreted by the court, and it was still unresolved at the time of the judgement. In desperation, we agreed to share the liability.

We were disappointed with our legal team and actively sought opinions from a new set of lawyers for the upcoming appeal. After an intensive search, we agreed upon Mr. Paul Starr of Mallesons Stephen Jaques. Paul recommended that we retain Simon Goodblatt as our Queen's Counsel, but as he was not allowed to practice in Hong Kong, because of the protection of local senior counsels, we met in Macao and in London. The barrister selected was Michael Thomas.

We applied for an appeal, and in the meantime, we approached both the marble factory and the bank about a possible settlement outside of court. They both refused. Both Heinz and I personally knew David Li, the general manager of the Bank of East Asia, so Heinz went to see him to see if there is any possibility of a settlement, but David avoided the issue, saying that he would leave it up to his lawyers. Our team prepared a very good case for the appeal. It was based on limitation, as we had already admitted to our breach of duty. It was a case of whether we could use the UK's or New Zealand's statute of limitations.

The appeal began on May 12, 1998. In an appeal, there are three judges to decide on the case. Our judges were Simon Mayo, Arthur Leong and Anthony Rogers. We did not have to be witnesses, as the lawyers would be arguing on the evidence from the first court case. I did attend one session during the presentation by Michael Thomas, but I found it full of legal terms and very boring, I don't think I could ever be a lawyer. We were in London on July 7, 1998, when I got a call from my secretary to announce that we had won the appeal. Good news. I sent a fax to Paul Starr and Michael Thomas to thank them for their efforts in winning the appeal.

Of course, the bank then took it to the Court of Final Appeal, so we kept the money that was returned in a fixed deposit, just in case we lost the final appeal. We kept the same legal team from the first appeal. This time, it was a case of strengthening our position regarding the argument on limitation. The final appeal was held in mid-March, 1999. The Court of Final Appeal consisted of Mr. Justice Litton, Justice Ching, Justice Bokhary, Justice Nazareth and Lord Nicholls of Birkenhead. Chief Justice Andrew Li abstained due to conflict of interest.

During the proceedings we were skiing in Lech, which had now become an annual event to celebrate our wedding anniversary. There wasn't much I could do even if I were to remain in Hong Kong. I expected that the judgement would come out in about two months, like the appeal, but months passed and it wasn't until seven months later, on December 10, 1999, when the judgement came out in our favour. What a relief! After three years of agony, it was now over and I could relax.

Reflecting on the way the law works, however, I find that litigation may not be the fairest way of settling cases. I felt, and still feel, that in our case, the main fault lay with the contractor and we were to blame in a minor way. Yet it ended up that the bank had to pay for everything. It's true that they inflated the figures, which represented the cost of replacing all the granite, when most of it was perfectly alright, but it was not their fault that the granite started to fall off. The reason why I think the contractor was primarily to blame is that we went out for tender, and it was part of the tender conditions that the tenderer had to provide the design of the fixing as well as the contract to supply materials and install them. When they won the tender, they brought in an expert from Italy who prepared the details for the fixing of the granite, and which the contractor followed.

We chose this method of tender as we felt we were not experienced enough with the new dry system of fixing the granite and had to rely upon the expertise of the suppliers, who had done this type of work before. I can now see that our fault lay in the fact that we should have checked the details more carefully against the British Standards, which gives certain guidelines for the fixing of stone. In-

248

stead, we relied only on the expertise of the supplier.

Nevertheless, all this was thrown out in the first trial and they concentrated on the interpretation of the statute of limitations instead. I find that in a court case, the outcome depends a great deal upon how skilled your solicitor is in preparing the case, how persuasive your barrister is in presenting the case and on the interpretation by the judge. If we had lost the case, we would have had to pay for the entire cost and the contractor would not be liable for anything. That would have been grossly unfair. From a moral point of view, say if the famous Bao Ching, the black-faced Judge Bao of Chinese folklore was to adjudicate, he probably would have ordered the contractor to repair the façade but not to re-clad the entire building and he would have ordered us to supervise the work at no cost to the bank. Although legally, we won the case—and I am very grateful for this—I do wonder if it was the fairest way to settle the problem.

JHK at home, 1999. (Photograph by Dr. Neville Poy.)

25

Our homes

During our entire married life in Hong Kong, we were fortunate enough to have lived in only three places—and each of them a house with a garden. Our first 32 years were spent in Ting Kau in the bungalow owned by Lana's father. We enjoyed being away from the crowded urban life in Hong Kong. We made many friends while living in Ting Kau, such as David and Jane Aker Jones, Steuart and Margaret Webb Johnston, Graham and Marie Barnes (now divorced), who were all former District Officers.

I commuted mostly on the ferry from Tsuen Wan to Central when our office was located in Prince's Building, but when the office moved to Wanchai, I started to drive, as I had a car park space in our office building. Evening engagements in town would become hectic, as I would have to pick Lana up from home. We therefore tried not to go out if we could help it.

All the children grew up in Ting Kau and they loved the environment. Although there was a school bus to take the children to school, it was hard on Lana to take them to other activities, such as lessons in swimming, piano, tennis and ballet. However, it was closer to the Beas River for their riding lessons. When the family sold the Ting Kau estate, we moved into our terrace house on Sassoon Road. It was only a 15-minute drive to town, so it was much more convenient. But by this time, the children were all studying abroad and the house was too big for the two of us.

We had a country house in a small village called Ta Ho Tun, just outside the town of Sai Kung in the eastern part of New Territories. We were very fortunate to get this property, as it was a waterfront lot, and we had only found it by pure luck.

One day, we were visiting our friend, an Italian artist Tony Casadei, who lived in the outskirts of Sai Kung. From his house, we spotted a site with an outcropping of rocks on the edge of the sea, so we sighed and remarked how nice it would be to have a house on that site. About a year later, Tony called us and excitedly told us that a site was for sale near to where we had spotted the outcropping of rocks. We immediately went to see the site, fell in love with it and bought it. The price was comparatively high at that time, but we were so anxious, we did not bargain. Now, it sounds like a bargain.

The property had two abandoned, broken-down houses on it, which suited us perfectly, as we planned to demolish them and build a new house. It came with some agricultural land, which we now use as extra parking space, and a kiln site detached from the house. The site had a southeast orientation and was right on the waterfront, with a stone pier at one end. It was perfect for our weekend house. Lana loved being close to water but did not enjoy getting seasick by slaving in the galley of a boat. She had always preferred having a house near the water rather than a boat on the water, and she now had her wish. The year was 1977.

The next step was a bit tricky. As this was a village house and under the jurisdiction of the District Office rather than the Building Authority, we went to the District Office to apply to build a new house. After months of negotiation, they finally said that we would have to apply for a surrender re-grant, which meant that we would have to surrender our benefits as villagers, such as paying token payments of rent to the government. We felt that we had been short-changed when the total area of the existing houses was 850 square feet but we were granted only 800 square feet during the exchange. Even though we no longer had the rights of a villager, they still imposed the building restrictions for village houses—specifically that each house could not be more than 700 square feet and could not exceed 25 feet in height. As we had a building area for 800 square feet, I designed a U-shaped building with a central courtyard, with each wing of the U forming an independent unit with a separate staircase, but adjacent to each other so we could knock the wall down later to make it into one house.

All the new village houses that were being built had a fake Spanish house look with a timid skirting of red tiles along the fringe of the roof. This was the solution of the Cathay Pacific pilots who first bought these village houses in Sai Kung; it was meant to give some character to offset the sterile effect caused by the restrictive village house-building regulations. This totally destroyed the look of the old Chinese village, which was traditionally comprised of two-storey houses with black tiled sloping roofs. As I wished to preserve this character, I designed the house with a pitched roof covered with black tiles, purchased from Japan.

The biggest challenge in retaining the pitched roof came from the height restriction of 25 feet. If I was to have only two storeys, it would be no problem, but we wanted more space, which necessitated a third floor. This was solved by lowering the ceilings of the rooms on the top floor and then having the slope of the roof rise as a parapet above the level of the 25-foot height limit. On one wing, however, the height was only two storeys in order to achieve a high ceiling for the living room. I felt it was worth the sacrifice in floor space to achieve the effect of a sloping roof. During this negotiation, the District Office was very obstructive, which made us suspect that there was more to the situation than inefficient ad-

ministration. It took over three years to finally sign the surrender re-grant agreement.

In 1982, we finished building the house. We then applied for a garden extension, which was granted in 1984, so we could build a swimming pool, which was finished in 1986. There was a leased land lot adjacent to the house, so we built a two-storey structure with garage space below and maids' quarters above. We kept it low as the owner of the house behind us insisted that we keep the same height as the previous structure so he could retain his view.

We were living on Sassoon Road and went every weekend to our country house in Sai Kung. It was a major effort to transport all the maids, the dogs, and the food for the weekend as well as maintaining the two houses. Lana finally felt that she could not continue to maintain two houses and asked me where I would prefer to live if we only had one place to live. I immediately said Sai Kung and so in 1998, we moved to Sai Kung as our permanent home and rented out our house on Sassoon Road. We then started to improve the house, adding this and that to make it more comfortable, and we developed the garden by adding a pavilion and a fishpond.

One day, Qi Gong, a renowned calligrapher and Wang Xi Xiang, a scholar and Ming furniture expert from Beijing, came to spend the day with us in Sai Kung. Qi Gong then named the house "Yat Siu Chou Tong," by putting our two first names together; Yat meaning first or Hajime and Siu meaning smile, the second character of Lana's Chinese name, and adding Chou Tong meaning a humble cottage. He wrote it in calligraphy and we had it carved on a piece of board, which is now proudly displayed above our red entrance gate.

In June of 1990, we attended Andrew's graduation from the Graduate School of Design at Harvard. He was later to graduate than Yuri as he first took an engineering degree at Tufts before he changed his mind and switched to architecture.

Pavilion in the garden, with a view of the fishpond beyond the moongate.

He worked for Moshe Safde and Ben Thompson before he came back to Hong Kong, and after working for various firms, including Tao and Kinoshita, he is now on his own doing factories in China and interior work. He married Lumen Man in November of 1994 at St. John's Cathedral and the reception was held at the Hong Kong Club. They now live in Sai Kung, close to us.

After graduating from MIT, Yuri decided to work in Boston and married Ted Sung, a fellow MIT student from Hawaii, in March 1991. We attended the wedding, which was held in Boston and attended mostly by her friends from the church, in which she was very actively involved. She now has three children and has become a full-time mother.

Reimi got married to Don Liu in March of 1995 at Christ Church in Kowloon Tong, her regular church, and the place where we got married 34 years ago. The reception was held at the Grand Hyatt and the dinner at the Hilton Hotel, before it got pulled down. After working for a private veterinarian practice, Reimi joined

View of our home from the pier with grandson, Jonathan, in the foreground.

Ocean Park and looks after marine mammals.

After graduating from Wellesley in 1992, Hiromi lived in New York and worked for J. J. Lally, a Chinese antique dealer. She learned a great deal about Chinese ceramics, bronze and jade under the tutorship of James Lally, and by constantly handling these items. After six years of working there, she felt that her capacity to learn was limited in the commercial area, so she went to Oxford for further studies in the field of Chinese Art, specializing in the Liao dynasty artefacts. We will definitely be attending her graduation ceremony for her PhD degree, as we missed her graduation ceremony at Wellesley.

Nanchansi in Wu Tai Shan, the earliest wooden building on record in China, built during the Tang Dynasty.

26

Travels

Lana and I have always been enthusiastic travellers, and over the years we have visited many fascinating and, sometimes, faraway places.

Our main interest has been travelling in China to explore the country's cultural background, in particular its artistic and architectural history. We have always made a point of seeing as many of the sites of ancient architecture, sculptures and paintings as possible. This interest took us to see the Buddhist sculptures at Luoyang, first visited in 1966 and again in 2000; to Yunkang in 1988; to Binglingsi, near Lanzhou, and Maijishan in 1995; and to see both classical and indigenous architecture at Beijing, Nanjing, Xian, Wutaishan, Chengede, Suzhou, Lijiang, Tibet, and Chaozhou.

In 1988, the Hong Kong Institute of Architects was planning a trip to Shanxi, to be led by Chung Wah Nan, but it got cancelled due to lack of interest. I was very disappointed, as I was keen to see Wu Tai Shan, so Lana and I, with Reimi, decided to take the trip ourselves, extending it to Datong. We took a train to

Taiyuan from Beijing and visited the Twin Pagoda Monastery, the symbol of Taiyuan; the Chongshan Monastery; and the Xuan Zhong Monastery, which was dramatically situated on the side of a mountain.

We left Taiyuan at 8 a.m. to go to Wu Tai Shan, one of the four sacred Buddhist mountains of China. In the afternoon, we got to the remote site of Nanchan Si by fording a stream with our jeep, as the bridge had been washed away in a recent flood. Located in a secluded valley, it is the most exquisite temple that I have ever seen. It was built in 782, during the early Tang dynasty, and is probably the oldest wooden structure in China; it is quite small, with only three bays and a gable and hip roof—simple in detail and beautifully proportioned. The earthquake of 1966 had destroyed it, but it was reconstructed piece by piece during the restoration of 1974-75. All except four of the original architectural supports were in good enough condition to be used in the restoration.

Close by is another Tang dynasty temple, the Foguang Si, built in 857. It is considered by many scholars of classical Chinese architecture to be the best example of Tang architecture. It is larger than Nanchan Si, with seven bays in width and four in length.It has a hip roof and huge imposing brackets supporting the wide overhanging eaves of the sweeping roof. The whole complex was built on three terraces with the main hall on the highest terrace.

Generally, Western architecture uses stone or brick, and Chinese architecture uses wood. Wood was plentiful in the old days, and with its availability and ease of construction, it continued to be the favoured building material. However, wood buildings can deteriorate with age and be easily destroyed by fire, and for this reason there are not many old wooden buildings remaining in China today. It is therefore rare that one finds surviving examples from the Tang dynasty.

From Wu Tai Shan, we travelled northwest to Datong, stopping by two very interesting buildings: the Hanging Monastery and a wooden pagoda. The Hanging Monastery is located on Mt. Hengshan and is unique in its setting. It literally hangs on the side of the cliff in a deep gorge, creating a dramatic sight. The walk along the fragile planks suspended from the cliff was a frightening experience. The Fogong Si Shijia Ta, was built in 1056 in the Liao dynasty and is the oldest wooden pagoda still existing in China. It is impressive in its size—216 feet in height and octagonal in shape with six layers of roof. It stands proudly alone in an open field, as all the other buildings of the monastery are gone. It is a must-see for any student of Chinese architecture.

Datong has many things to see, the most famous of which are the series of cave sculptures at Yungang. Started in the Northern Wei dynasty, it has a wealth of superb Buddhist sculptures carved into 53 caves and niches; the largest is a 17-metre sitting Buddha. I was very impressed with the quality of the Northern Wei and Tang sculptures in these caves. The carvings are well executed and probably better preserved than those at Luoyang. Besides the Yungang caves, we also saw several important temples of the later Liao and Jin periods.

Later, we started to join groups led by Professor P. P. Ho, a professor of architecture at the Chinese University, who conducted tours of outstanding cultural remains, usually those located at inconvenient and difficult places to get to. For us it was an ideal arrangement to see these treasures in remote places in relative comfort and not have to worry about catching the next bus or hiring an expensive car. P. P. Ho was very knowledgeable about Chinese Buddhist art and architecture, and he would not only concentrate on areas of significance or influence but would also patiently explain the features that made them significant.

One such trip was to Ningxia in 2000, organized by the Friends of the Hong Kong Museum of Art. We covered the area between Yinchuan, the capital of Ningxia, to Xian, following the northern route of the Silk Road. In and around Yinchuan, we mostly saw remains of the Western Xia kingdom (1038-1227) formed by the Tanguts, a Tibetan tribe, through an alliance with the Khi-

Group at the twin pagodas at Baisikou, Ningxia.

tans of the Liao dynasty against their common foe, the Sungs, until their destruction by the Mongols in 1227. The remains of their Buddhist pagodas and royal tombs, made of rammed earth, bear silent testimony to their civilization.

South of Yinchuan, in Qingtongxia County, on the eastern slope of a mountain, there stands an interesting structure with 108 pagodas, built during the Yuan dynasty, and arranged in 12 rows forming the shape of a triangle. A reservoir was built there so we had to take a boat, but by the time we arrived, it was late afternoon with the sun behind the hill, making it very difficult to take good photographs in the glare.

In Zhongwei, going south, we saw a most exuberant baroque Chinese building called Gaomiao Temple. It is used by three religions—Buddhism, Taoism and Confucianism—and has more than 260 rooms, set on a compact site. This multi-storey structure is full of pavilions piled on top of each other with robust upturned eaves, creating a rich symphony of forms. It is almost like Bach's music transformed into architecture—a wonderful surprise.

We also saw mosques along the route, as 40 percent of Ningxia's four million inhabitants are Huis—of the Islamic faith. Most of the recent ones were done in the Islamic style but the one in Tongxin was done in the style of classical Chinese architecture. The building gave a feeling of solemn dignity with its greyish brown colour and solidity.

The evidence of the Silk Road manifested itself at the Xumishan Grottos, with more than 300 statues of Buddha, from the Northern Wei to the Tang dynasties, carved into the mountain. Out of the 135 caves only 13 are intact. Some of the sculptures are in good condition, especially the superb 20-metre-high seated Maitreya. These sculptures are scattered along a dry, almost bare rocky mountainside, so we had to select carefully to reach those accessible within our limited time. It was worth seeing the isolated cave number 105 with its Tang sculptures. It was also interesting to see the effect of Buddhism in this part of the Silk Road. Additionally, at the museum at Guyuan, near the Xumishan Grottos, we saw many items from the Silk Road: a fine Roman vase with naked figures hammered out, hundreds of miniature clay figures used for burial, Tang figures and bronze Buddhas.

At Qingyan, there were three grottos to see. One contained a superb Tang relief of Buddha sitting on a huge elephant. Closer to Xian, at Binxian, was a big Buddha, from the Tang dynasty, which was restored in the Qing dynasty and was quite ugly. It was housed in a brick structure with a temple above it where one could walk up to look face-to-face at the big Buddha—a rather crude way of displaying the sculpture.

From Xian, we visited some more cave sculptures, the Yaowangshan

At Sichuan, Leshan – giant Buddha (Maitreya), newly repainted, 71 meters high, from the Tang Dynasty. Back row (left to right): Jennifer Welch, Nancy Thompson, Lana, Roger Moss, Veryai Bradshaw, Chris Hall, Ina Ng, JHK, Kaye Shu. Front row (left to right): P.P. Ho, Barbara Park, Piper Tseng, Ingrid Lam.

Sculpture (dating 1179-1249) at Bao Ding Shao, Dazu, Szechuan.

Grottos with mostly Tang dynasty sculptures. A different kind of stone was used, giving a black sheen to the sculptures when they were polished. Surprisingly, they were not damaged at all. All in all, this was a very interesting trip into a part of China rarely visited, revealing excellent remains of Buddhist sculptures.

The next trip with P. P. Ho was in May of 2001 from Chongqing to Chengdu, in Szechuan province to see those remote cave sculptures hidden in the valleys where

Buddhism once exerted an influence. Because of their out-of-the way location, most of these sculptures were not damaged by the Red Guards. Our itinerary included: Dazu, where Professor Ho gave us a lecture on Buddhist iconography; Anyue, an isolated part of Sichuan; Rongxian, which has the second largest Buddha in China—37 metres high; and Leshan, where the world's largest Buddha rises majestically 71 metres above the river. We also visited Emei Shan, one of the four sacred mountains of Buddhism. At the time, it was particularly beautiful, covered with rhododendrons in full bloom. At the summit, where we visited Jingding Monastery, we were enthralled to view a halo around the sun, which is considered auspicious. Thinking back on it, I look forward to many more trips with P. P. Ho to see other areas of rich cultural interest in China.

In the summer of 2000, we decided to try a different kind of travel adventure, an exploration-type cruise to the North Pole. I had seen a magazine advertisement for a trip to the North Pole on a Russian icebreaker, sponsored by the American Museum of Natural History in New York. I immediately wrote to them for further details.

Lana was not too keen on going unless she had company, so we asked Loretta and Raymond Lunney, with whom we had taken a trip to the Panama Canal, to join us. I had always wanted to go to the North Pole and the Antarctic and to take the Northwest Passage, so this was a step in the right direction. Unlike the South Pole, there is no land at the North Pole. It is a permanent cover of ice that is constantly moving. If you were to place a pole on the ice at North Pole today, it would have drifted three miles by the next day. If there is really nothing there, why go? Like the reason for climbing Mt. Everest, the answer is: because it is there.

From 1894 to 1914, seventeen brave explorers attempted the journey and failed; among them were two Americans using dog sleds—Frederick Cook in

1908, and Robert Peary in 1909, who claimed to be the first, which was widely believed. In fact, the North Pole was finally reached in 1948, when the Russians landed by aircraft. By surface, it was not until 1968 that an American, Ralph Plaisted, and three others reached the pole on a snow scooter from Canada, and then flew home. By sea, it was not until 1977, with the development of nuclear-powered icebreakers, that the Russians were able to reach the North Pole. By the time we went on the expedition, a total of 3,700 people had travelled by icebreakers to the North Pole, with 5,800 more reaching the spot by submarine, aircraft, helicopter and various means on the surface.

As we were starting the journey at Oslo, we decided to go to Helsinki first to see the buildings of Alvar Aalto. We next flew to Oslo, saw the Folksmuseum and Viking Ship Museum, then took a long walk to the Fram Museum. The latter was very interesting as it displayed the ship that Fram had built to resist the pressure of ice and to prove his theory that the ice in the Arctic Ocean, above Russia, flows from east to west. He used this ship to test his theory, and he got close to, but was unsuccessful in reaching, the North Pole.

It was a three-and-half hour flight from Oslo to Longyearbyen on Svalbard, a barren looking place with only 1,000 residents in the summer. It is on the edge of a shallow harbour surrounded by bare mountains and is well within the Arctic Circle. After a tour of the town, we transferred to our ship, *Yamal*, by a 20-person helicopter, which took half an hour. Since the ship was nuclear powered, it was not allowed to dock in the harbour so we had to board by helicopters. There were 46 passengers on board, plus scientists and lecturers from Harvard, MIT, U of Michigan and the Scott Polar Research Institute, along with their wives.

Painted bright red, the ship looked more like a freighter than a cruiser. At 150 metres long, and reinforced by two inches of armoured steel on the outer hull, it was built to cut through five metres of ice. It certainly looked like a sturdy

James and Lana
at the North Pole.

ship that could withstand the worst ice conditions. It had two helicopters on board, a large 20-passenger one for transporting people and a smaller one to carry out surveys on ice conditions.

During our entire four-day trip out, the sun never set as we headed toward the North Pole. At first, it was open sea, but we soon hit the ice and then the ship zigzagged through the open cracks in the ice. We soon got used to the sunlight and the tremendous crushing sound of the ice when we were trying to sleep. During the day, we would have lectures, such as Robert Headland from the Scott Polar Research Institute at Cambridge on "Unveiling the Arctic" or James McCarthy of Harvard on "The Role of Ice in Polar Ecosystems." If there were things of interest on the ice, the Captain would make an announcement and everyone would go out on deck. The first day out, we saw a mother polar bear with two cute cubs, about two or three years old, trailing behind her. They were curious and playful, and when the boat stopped to observe them, they came right up to the boat to investigate. As we got closer to the Pole, however, there were no birds or any other living creatures.

One day, the crew dressed up like King Neptune and his followers and held court where the Captain had to seek permission to proceed to the North Pole. After the ceremony, we had an outdoor barbeque lunch of Austrian sausages and sauerkraut. The food was very good, catered by an Austrian group, but the waiters and waitresses were Russians.

On the fourth day, at 10:22 p.m., we reached the North Pole, and we were all amazed to see open water. The temperature was 1 degree C, the warmest it has ever been in the North Pole. James McCarthy said that when he had come to the North Pole two years ago, the ice was two metres thick. Now it was only one metre thick and in open sea at that. When he got back home, James wrote in the *New York Times* of this warming at the North Pole.

The next morning, the ship stopped in the middle of the solid ice so we could step onto it and celebrate our arrival at the North Pole. It was a bright and sunny day with a temperature of –5 degrees C. After champagne and caviar for breakfast on the ice, we took group photos of the different organizations that were on the expedition. The crew stuck a sign in the ice saying North Pole 90N, and some brave people took the polar plunge—that is, jumping into the freezing water.

We then headed back, and it took three days to get to Franz Josef Land, the northernmost islands of Russia. At Franz Josef Land, we took helicopters to Cape Norway to observe the hut where the explorer Nansen rested after he failed to reach the North Pole. The stone walls and the ridgepole were still there. He had put walrus skins on top to make the hut bear proof. The beach was rocky with small stones, covered in lichens and small flowers, and surrounded by huge mountains, bare with streaks of snow. The Russian guards kept a wary eye on us. Later we passed by Rubini Rock, a huge volcanic outcropping with thousands of birds nesting—gulls, murre, fulmars, and more.

At 8:00 p.m. that evening, we took the helicopter to Cape Flora on Rudolfa Island to see the remains of huts left behind by Arctic explorers and adventurers. As we got closer to Svalbard, there were fewer ice floes, and we saw seals and whales. We had a review session by all the lecturers, who spoke on the warming at the North Pole and the thinning of the ice there. The final evening, the Russian crew gave a show, which was very funny. The Russians can have a great sense of humour.

This cruise was completely different and much more rewarding than any other that I had ever taken. It was small and friendly, and we got to know everyone and share our mutual interest in exploring different parts of the globe. I would like to do the Antarctic, but listening to the tales of the rough crossing at Drake Channel and getting seasick put Lana's enthusiasm off. I hope I can convince her that crossing the Bering Sea for the Northwest Passage would be much better.

In 2001 we joined a Stanford Alumni Association trip on the famous pilgrimage walk to Santiago de Compostela in Northern Spain. When I heard that David Hart, a Stanford alumnus, did this walk in the previous year, I expressed my interest and he helped us join the Alumni Association, even though we were not Stanford graduates. I had heard a great deal about this walk and had always

Stanford group at the west façade of the
cathedral at Santiago de Campostella.

wanted to try it, but now that we are older and used to comfort, to walk the
whole length of 500 miles would have been too strenuous, even though Shirley
MacLaine did it in her 60s. This excursion offered a perfect opportunity to walk
the most interesting or typical parts of the road in pleasant company, to enjoy
good food, to stay at some of the most special and comfortable *paradors,* and to
experience and appreciate the many examples of Romanesque churches. Do it in
style, as they say.

Climb from Villa Franca to O Cebreiro.

The whole trip took 14 days with 29 participants, all Americans (except for Lana and me), accompanied by Emily Casperson from the Alumni and Prof. Brad Gregory from Stanford, who gave lectures relating to the pilgrimage. Peter Watson, who led the walk, was not only knowledgeable about the history and architecture of places we visited, but he was also an efficient organizer, looking after the logistics of excellent picnic lunches, hotels, dinners, selection of wine and all transport. The walk began on the French side of the Pyrenees at the small village of St. Jean Pied de Port and continued westward along the northern part of Spain through Burgos and Leon to finish at Santiago de Compostela.

The symbol of the road to Santiago is the scallop shell, like the Shell gasoline sign. All along the way, we would follow the sign of the scallop or the yellow arrow indicating the right path. Many walkers would carry a staff and the shell as a sign of pilgrimage. Our trip started on June 19 and included visits to several locales of religious or historical importance. These included: the monument to Roland at Roncesvalles, Spain; Pamplona of Hemingway, bull-running and cathedral fame; the famous medieval pilgrims' bridge of Puenta de la Reina; numerous Romanesque churches; Sahagun, where there is a fine example of Mudejar Romanesque architecture; and the beautiful cathedral town of Leon.

After several days of travelling, sometimes on foot, sometimes by bus, we approached Santiago de Campostela. We had our last picnic lunch in the shade of a forest beside a small stream. We then drove to the outskirts of Santiago to walk the final mile or two along the crooked streets of Santiago, well trodden by centuries of pilgrims. At the cathedral we followed the usual ritual of all the pilgrims, entered by the north gate, hugged the statue of St. James behind the altar and went down to the crypt to see his remains. What we did not do was register as having officially walked the whole route, as we had only walked parts of it. We spent two nights at the splendid Parador de los Reyes Catolicos, located right next to the cathedral, and built at the end of the 15th century as a pilgrim hospital. That evening, we walked to Restaurant Vilar where we had a very good meal of scallops and hake. We all received the shell of the scallop as a sign of our achievement.

We spent the final day looking at the cathedral and exploring the city on our own. The cathedral is one of the masterpieces of Spanish Romanesque architecture; inside is the impressive Portico of Glory, a Romanesque gate with a seated sculpture of St. James on top of the central mullion. A huge incense burner swung under the dome, placed there especially for our benefit. We attended the morning service, and the priest welcomed our group as he did other pilgrims. We had arrived. That evening, we had our farewell dinner in the hotel, where we exchanged addresses and telephone numbers.

The next day, we flew back to London. I threw away my worn-out Austrian hiking boots, as they were falling apart. I took my walking stick as a souvenir. We had walked 53 miles out of a total of 500 miles through the plains, the forest, villages and towns, up and down mountains, crossing numerous rivers, visiting many churches, monasteries, and castles. We learned about Romanesque architecture and sculpture and tasted wonderful Navaresse food along the way. I wish I could have appreciated the local wine but the doctor warned me not to touch wine. I did not have any religious revelations or meditate or dream as Shirley Maclaine did, but nevertheless it was a deeply enriching experience.

In the summer of 2002, Hiromi, Lana and I took a 10-day musical river cruise from St. Petersburg to Moscow. We went to St. Petersburg a day earlier in order to take in the musical festival of the White Nights. After we checked in at the Grand Hotel Europe, we walked along Nevsky Prospect, the Fifth Avenue of St. Petersburg. As we were making our way to the department store, a man in a plaid jacket rudely cut across Lana and I, separating us. Immediately, Lana sensed something was wrong and checked her handbag and, sure enough, her wallet was missing. The man disappeared and it happened so fast, we didn't have time to react. We immediately went back to the hotel to report the loss of a credit card. Fortunately, she was not carrying much cash, as we had just arrived. What a unpleasant way to start a trip.

The next day things looked up, and at the Hermitage Museum, the curator was kind enough to open parts of the museum closed to the public. We concentrated on the collection of Central Asia and China, a viewing arranged through contacts of Omi. That evening, we walked to Mariiensky Theatre to see the ballet Le Corsaire. After the ballet, the car came to pick us up to check into our ship, *Viking Pakhomov*. Our cabin was very comfortable; it was more like a junior suite, combining two regular rooms into one. Besides a large double bed, it had a

Lana and Hiromi (with Ms. Pakhomov) taking a Russian River cruise.

sofa and desk, still allowing space to move around.

The next two days, we toured St. Petersburg before setting sail on the evening of the second day. We returned to the Hermitage to see the usual high-lights, such as Rembrandt, Leonardo and Van Dyke. I was surprised at the ex-cellent collection of impressionists and the works of Matisse and Picasso. It was fortunate that we had seen the works of Central Asia and China independently the day before, as we wouldn't otherwise have had the time. After dinner on the ship, we bussed out to hear a private concert in the reception room of Menshikov Palace where Peter the Great used to give his parties. The next day, we visited the Peter and Paul Fortress, where the Romanovs were buried, and later drove to Peterhof, a summer palace built by Peter the Great and fashioned after Versailles. I liked the gardens of Peterhof better than Versailles; I was especially taken with the ornate waterfall tumbling down from the palace to the garden, before disappearing into the Gulf of Finland.

We started our journey upstream on the Neva River and headed toward Lake Ladoga and the Svir River.

Life on the ship was quite busy, and we stopped off at various places to sightsee and take in churches, farmhouses, monasteries and museums. As this was supposed to be a musical tour, we also visited many places of musical interest, such as the homes of Rimsky Korsakov and Tchaikovsky; we attended special concerts in St. Petersburg and performances of folk dances and songs; we also heard local choral music and the ringing of church bells along the way. The Russians are superb at choral singing, which apparently developed because they were not allowed to use musical instruments in their churches. We were also entertained by John Amis, a radio commentator on music, who gave lectures on many kinds of music. He was funny at times but a bit too old, as he fumbled over an antiquated tape recorder that never seemed to work properly. The last evening before we reached Moscow, the Russian crew gave a boisterous show, which was rather entertaining. One evening they showed the film *Rasputin*, which prompted me to read the book, *Nicholas and Alexandra*, by Robert Massie. It proved that the interpretation in the film was pretty accurate. During the cruise, I was reading the book *Peter the Great*, also by Robert Massie, which helped me to understand the history of many places that we visited.

In Moscow, we were taken on a tour of the city, ending at the Red Square. We went into GUM and bought some Russian caviar; Lana had attended a lecture on caviar on the cruise and knew exactly what to buy. We saw two ballets at the Bolshoi for the two evenings we were there. The first was *Giselle*, which we did not think was very good, and the second night was the *Magic Flute*, which I had thought was an opera. The second day, we visited the Kremlin to see the Church of Assumption and the museum at the Armoury, where Lana was keen to see the

Fabergé eggs.

We enjoyed the river cruise, probably more than any ocean-going cruise. The river ships are small and carry fewer people than ocean liners, so the opportunity to meet other people and make friends is much greater. There was the added advantage that we never got seasick, a very important point for Lana. Such cruises are also convenient, docking right at the places of interest—no tenders, no lining up to disembark, no waiting. Usually, we could return at our leisure as long as we got back before the ship sailed. We will be planning more river tours from now on—as we look forward to many more years of indulging our love for travel.

40th Wedding Anniversary at the Hotel Post, Lech. Clockwise from the left: Don, Reimi, JHK, Lana, Andrew, Lumen and Hiromi.

Epilogue: The joys of life

We celebrated our 40th anniversary in 2001 by inviting all the children with their families to Lech, and to join us later on our second honeymoon. Andrew with his wife Lumen, Reimi with her husband Don, and Hiromi came, but Yuri and her family could not make it, as it was during their children's school term. We spent one week together in Lech skiing and celebrating our anniversary. We then flew to Lyon to drive around Auvergne, as part of our second honeymoon trip. Hiromi suggested that we spend our second honeymoon retracing our original honeymoon trip. We tried to cover parts of it by going back to Munich and then to St. Anton; we then did the drive around the Auvergne area, which we wanted to see because we had bypassed it on our first honeymoon.

We flew from Lyon to Rome and did a tour of Umbria, revisiting many of the places we had visited on our first honeymoon. The difference between this honeymoon and our first one is that we were able to stay in comfortable hotels and to dine in Michelin two- and three-starred restaurants, which we couldn't afford on our first honeymoon.

However, the fresh excitement and simple joy that we experienced on our first honeymoon was lacking. Before, we would buy a baguette and cheese to picnic beside a stream; this time, we would stop at a comfortable restaurant for our lunch. It had once meant so much to us to count our pennies to buy some flowers or to have a cup of coffee, whereas now, the cost does not even occur to us. As one matures and becomes more affluent, the simple things in life are taken for granted and lose their innocent joy.

Our joy in life now is from the family and from our travels. Our annual travel schedule has now settled down to a certain pattern. We usually spend January and February in Hong Kong, when the weather is nice and cool for hikes in the country park around our home in Sai Kung. Chinese New Year, which falls within these two months, is celebrated quietly at home as most of the people travel out of Hong Kong to take advantage of the long public holiday. In March, we fly to London for a few days before going to Lech, in Austria, to ski for two weeks and to celebrate our wedding anniversary. We have been going back to Lech for the past 17 years. Before we fly to Vancouver to celebrate my mother's birthday on April 21, we take a tour or a cruise somewhere in Europe, retracing our honeymoon trip of 2001, or we take a cruise such as the one in 2004, with Zegrahm on the Atlantic— from Dakar to Verde Island, the Canary Islands, Morocco, Gibraltar and Spain, to disembark at Lisbon. From Vancouver, we return home, completing a round-the-world tour.

In June, we go to London again, spending two or three months in Europe to escape the heat and humidity of Hong Kong. An exception was made in 2004, when we spent the summer in Whistler, Canada, with our grandchildren, and again in 2005 when Yuri's family came to Hong Kong to spend their school holidays with us. Using London as our base, we drive to the splendid gardens in Britain with Lana's cousins, Dum Dum and Samn Lim, or we take a river cruise down the Danube to the Black Sea, or we simply enjoy walking and eating in

July 2004 at Whistler. Back row, left to right: Aki, Yuri, Sonya, Reimi. Front row, left to right: Mother, Michelle, Leilani, JHK.

Venice or Paris.

Autumn in Hong Kong is the best time of the year. It is sunny without being too hot or humid and it rarely rains. We enjoy visiting places in Asia during this time; for example, in 2005, we went to Tokyo and to an *onsen* in Hakone, took a tour of Thailand with the Oriental Ceramic Society, had a short visit to Ho Chi Minh City and went to Beijing to celebrate the 55th reunion of Lana's class at Pui Ching.

As one gets older, getting together as a family becomes more and more important. All the children are adults now, with families of their own, and they are scattered all over the world. In no time, their children will become adults and will go their own ways. We have always wanted to keep the family as close as possible,

July 2005, JHK and Lana at home with grandchildren, Jonathan, Michelle, Leilani and Sonya.

and one way of doing this is to get together often.

We started off by taking Yuri's family on a Disney Cruise in the Carib-
bean in 2002. It was a great success, enjoyed not only by the children, but also
by the adults. The next time, in 2004, we decided to get all the grandchildren
together at Whistler. It would also give the grandchildren a chance to get to know
their great grandmother, who lives in Vancouver. We rented a house large enough
to accommodate Yuri and her family, Reimi and her family, Omi and ourselves;
and we took a maid with us to do the housework. We walked along the forest
trail, saw bears, which greatly excited the children, went bicycling around the
lake, and swam in the indoor pool. It was exhausting, but fun.

In 2005, Yuri's family came to Hong Kong to spend three weeks with us during the summer holidays; this enabled all the grandchildren to get together. We felt it would be less strenuous to stay in our home with the help of maids. There is currently no need for Reimi's family nor Andrew's family to travel, as they all live in Hong Kong. However, because of the heat and humidity of Hong Kong, the long flight from Boston and the 12-hour time difference with its inevitable jet lag, it does not seem to be a good idea to be in Hong Kong for the summer in the future. Therefore, for 2006, we are planning to get together in England where the weather is kinder (although it could be wet). It is closer to Boston and we plan to be in London anyway.

Though I am now absorbed in my family life and travel plans, I still take time to reflect on my professional life and all that it has meant to me over the years.

As an architect, I participated in the height of the building boom in Hong Kong, contributing to the skyline of the city. It was a very exciting time for me, riding not only on the crest of development, but also surviving the low period during the riots of 1967 by expanding abroad. There was a great satisfaction in reviving our activities in China, a new frontier, and I am pleased to see that the firm is doing so well in China today.

I enjoyed my professional life tremendously; if I were to live my life again, I would choose architecture. When students ask me what advice I can give them, I reply, "Enjoy your work."

I certainly did.

Printed in the United States
By Bookmasters